Movie Blogs II

William Behr Mueller

William Behr Mueller

Also by the author

Operation Belize

Four in a Row

Goonie's Ghost

Peter Monocot and the Sea Devils

Massacre at Fort Sage

Sweet Drop in Africa: Hope

Sweet Drop in Africa: Charity

Sweet Drop in Africa: Faith

Akasha

Duel at Sea

Ishmael's Quest

Taking Care of Business

Silent Edge

Herlong

Looking for Jack: Massacre at Fort Sage 2

Murder at the Ritz Carlton

So You Want to Fix It

Dive to the Deep Six

Rider and other stories

The Book of Astaroth

Celestial Moon

Book Blogs

Ozimund's Quest

Frizzimund's Quest

Jerrimund's Quest

Murder on the California Zephyr: A Herlong Novel

Movie Blogs

Antique Bazaar: An Echoes of Korea Love Story

Duel at Sea II

Probe: The Movie

Movie World

Movie World 2

Table of Contents

William Behr Mueller

3:10 to Yuma

After fifty years this tripartite production updates and improves the previous version that starred Glenn Ford as Ben Wade.

This film opens with William Evans (Logan Lerman) trying to read a western dime novel in bed. He snuffs his match as his father, Dan Evans (Christian Bale) and his mother Alice Evans (Gretchen Mol) hear something and that something is their barn burning.

Dan, a leg amputee from the Civil War, and William run to the barn to try to save the horses and tack before the entire building goes up in flames.

As the Evans are trying to rationalize the destruction of the barn, Ben Wade (Russell Crowe) and his gang wait for an armored stage (Gatling gun and bounty hunters) with the money box. Wade shows his artistic ability by sketching a beautiful raptor as his second in command Charlie Prince (Ben Foster) is eager to take the stage and the money.

Dan and his sons leave the farm to go round up their cattle. William wants to take revenge on the man responsible for the barn burning but Dan puts him off.

Wade's gang attacks the stage and kills most of the guards. Byron McElroy (Peter Fonda) is the last of the lawmen/bounty men to escape the fury of the Wade gang. As Prince administers the coup de grace to some of the men who were only wounded he spies McElroy and shoots him in the belly. Wade comes over and tells McElroy he will not kill him like that.

William Behr Mueller

Dan and his sons view the spectacle of the destroyed stage and the wounded and killed men. One of the lawmen takes a gang member hostage and tells Wade and his gang that he will kill the man if they attempt to kill him. Wade assesses the situation and then kills his own gang member and the lawman.

Wade discovers Evans and his sons and takes their horses saying they will get them back in due course.

After Wade and the gang leave Evans discovers McElroy and makes a travois to take him to Bisbee. Shortly they find the horses that Wade took from them and then Evans tells his boys to round up the cattle as he takes McElroy to get medical help.

In the meantime, Wade and Prince have entered Bisbee and take over the town. Wade finds the barmaid attractive and beds her. He also draws a sketch of her nude backside a la some of the European painters of the time.

Prince lures the lawmen out of town and they finally find Dan Evans and McElroy and also find out that the Wade gang is probably in Bisbee. The lawmen ride hell for leather back to town.

Wade is captured and Evans demands $200.00 to help take Wade to Contention where he will board the train to the prison in Yuma.

The group returns to Evans' spread to wait for the stage that contains Wade. With great caution one of the lawmen exchanges places with Wade. The others take Wade into the house.

The ruse of having a lawman with Ben Wade's signature hat on board the stage is predicated on the stage reaching the fort before the rest of Wade's gang can intercept it.

As the men and Wade eat dinner, Wade makes a play for Evans' wife. She is taken by how different he is from what she's been led to believe him to be. Dan Evans tells her to forget about Wade. She tries to dissuade him from accompanying the men to take Wade to the train for Yuma.

Dan and the other men leave the spread and ride as far as they can before they have to make camp. Unknown to Dan his son William had left the ranch and is following them. One of the men who burned down Evans' barn torments Wade telling him that he could have been sleeping in a soft bed instead of the ground. Shortly, Wade attacks and kills the man with a fork that he purloined from the Evans' table.

McElroy severely beats Wade because of his killing the lawman. He also discounts having to bury the man saying that they might as well dig graves for all of them.

The group leaves the camp and then they decide to take a shortcut through apache country to avoid being caught by Wade's gang.

Wade attacks McElroy and takes his shotgun. He throws McElroy off a cliff. He appears to have the upper hand when William Evans shows up and demonstrates that he will shoot Wade if he doesn't put the gun down.

In the meantime, Prince finds the ruse of the lawman with Ben Wade's hat and burns him alive before they backtrack to catch up with the other lawmen and Ben Wade.

William Behr Mueller

Three apaches attack the group. Wade takes Dan Evans gun and kills the apaches and then demands the keys to his handcuffs. He takes the horses and leaves Evans and the other men. They decide to trail him because as Dan Evans says, "There ain't no reward for getting' him halfway…"

Wade enters a Chinese construction camp and tries to get his handcuffs removed. The lawman recognizes Wade and captures him. The gang boss tortures Wade because Wade killed his son.

Wade and the lawmen that have finally caught up with him disable the construction gang and ride away after blowing up the exit to the tunnel. The doctor is wounded in the fray and dies.

Evans and Wade and the others arrive in Contention, the train depot. Wade and the others take the bridal suite as they wait for the train.

Prince and the rest of Wade's gang arrive at the Chinese construction site. Prince kills the gang boss and his men because after they admit to being a posse, Prince says "I hate posses."

In the bridal suite, Wade attempts to bribe Evans with $1,000.00. Evans refuses.

Grayson Butterfield (Dallas Roberts) brings the local marshal and his boys to make sure that Wade gets on the train.

Prince and the others arrive in Contention. He offers $200.00 cash money to any man willing to shoot the men guarding Wade. The changing odds make the marshal decide to bow out. It does him and the others no good as Prince and the rest of the gang kill them all.

Dan Evans decides to go it alone after making a bargain with Butterfield to take his son back to the ranch.

The tension mounts as the hour for the train approaches. Shooters abound throughout the town as Wade sketches.

Outside the hotel a general gunfight ensues. Prince appears to protect Wade by shooting some of the men he recruited with the promise of the two hundred dollars.

Wade and Evans fight and Evans confesses the circumstances of how he lost his leg. Wade eases up and doesn't kill Evans. They escape over the roofs of the buildings.

William sees the sketch of his father that Wade drew.

Wade helps Evans escape his own gang. They make it inside the train station. Both men share some of their background.

The 3:10 finally arrives—late.

Wade gets on the train and then Prince kills him. William watches this horror and then Wade gets his guns and kills Prince and other members of his gang who are within gunshot range. He finally becomes friends with Dan Evans.

William aims his pistol at Wade and then relents as he looks at his dead father.

Wade climbs aboard the trains and gives his guns to the train guard. He also whistles for his horse, which follows the train and ends the film.

If you're a fan of high quality acting, high quality adventure and high quality action then you will enjoy this film.

12 Angry Men

You wonder why these men are angry. The reason behind the title becomes quite clear during the first few minutes of the film.

An establishing shot tilts to show the inscription on a courthouse. Inside various people move about. The men of the title sit in a jury box and a very tired judge gives them the instructions about what they are about to do in the jury room. He also says that there will be no modification of the sentence. If they find the defendant guilty the death penalty is mandatory.

The jurors leave the courtroom and enter the jury room for their deliberations.

(Though the actors are identified by their juror numbers I shall use their stage names) Martin Balsam takes command of the proceeding and seats the jurors in the same order as their numbers. They take a vote and it is eleven guilty to one not guilty. The one is Henry Fonda. One of the most outspoken of the jurors (Lee J. Cobb) immediately wants to know why Fonda is the only hold-out. Fonda says he just wants to talk about the case. That response infuriates Cobb who asks what there is to talk about. Fonda says that before he votes to put a man to death he wants to talk about the case.

Jack Warden has tickets for a ball game and is very impatient to get the verdict settled. Another very vociferous juror is Ed Begley who not only is sure that the kid who supposedly murdered his father is guilty but is "one of those" who will always lie to protect himself.

Another of the jurors (Jack Klugman) tells Begley that he grew up in the slums and that all the people there are not the kind that will maraud the rest of society.

Balsam has a hard time keeping the men focused on the verdict.

After Fonda is pilloried for his stand and some of the reasons he's presented to poke holes in the prosecution's case, he finally makes a proposition: If in a secret vote there is no not guilty he will bend to the will of the majority.

The men vote and Balsam reads the results. There is one not guilty vote.

Cobb immediately goes ballistic and accuses Klugman of being the not guilty vote. They almost come to blows before Joseph Sweeney reveals the fact that he is the not guilty vote. Cobb berates him for changing his vote and then Sweeney has to say that he did so to give Fonda more time to talk about the case.

Balsam asks the bailiff to get the murder weapon for them. They examine the weapon. Cobb sticks it into the table. Fonda replies to the dramatic gesture by pulling out an identical switch blade knife and sticking it beside the murder weapon. He is berated for breaking the law by buying the knife.

Balsam returns the murder weapon to the bailiff.

E.G. Marshall appears to be the soul of reason in the group as he emphasizes the fact that when the young man was arrested he couldn't name the movie he was supposed to be at and that no one saw him either leave or come back to the apartment where the murder occurred.

William Behr Mueller

Warden sweats like the rest of the men, except for Marshall who says he doesn't sweat. Warden continues to make jokes trying to get the rest of them to come to a verdict so he can get out to the ballgame.

Fonda continues to examine the prosecution's case, particularly the one eye witness who stated that she saw the murder occur. She did this by tossing and turning in her bed until an elevated train passed by through which she was able to see the defendant plunge the knife into his father.

Fonda uses the diagram of the other witness' apartment to lay out in the room the distances shown in the diagram. He then asks John Fiedler to time him as he mimics the walk of the old man who heard the defendant yell he would kill his father after which he heard the body thump the floor.

The 15-second interval testified to by the old man turns out to be 41-seconds as stepped off by Fonda.

Cobb continues to shout at them for wasting time when they have an eyewitness. Marshall also points out the fact that the defendant couldn't remember any details of the movies he was supposedly to have seen.

Fonda grills Marshall about what he did for the past few days and finds out that he misremembered the title of one of the movies that he and his wife saw. Fonda scores points because Marshall was under no duress and couldn't remember the exact title of the movie.

After another couple of votes, the count is six guilty, six not guilty. Begley adds to the shouting match until all of the men turn their backs on him and he is forced to take the dunce's chair away from the juror table.

More not guilty votes appear and finally Cobb is the lone holdout, reversing Fonda's position at the start of the film.

Cobb makes a move toward Fonda and has to be restrained. He tells the rest of them that he doesn't have to account for his guilty vote.

They stare him down and finally he reveals that it is the breakup with his son that has caused his anger.

With his head in his hands, Cobb finally says "not guilty."

The men leave the jury room.

Outside, Sweeney asks Fonda what his name is. Fonda tells him and Sweeney says he'll see him around.

Cobb is the last to leave and we see him in a long shot apparently dejected by the experience.

All the men are given cameo shots at the end of the film to identify them.

If you want a very lively jury room deliberation with great dialog and intense performances then you will get your fill with this film.

Apocalypse Now

Coppola opens his film with a shot of tightly packed palm trees with a helicopter passing through the frame. Soon the sweaty face of Captain Willard (Martin Sheen) montages with the attack on the village protected by the palms.

Willard is in a hotel room in Saigon drinking and soon to experience what will become known as Post Traumatic Stress Syndrome. His recollections and inability to resolve them lead him to a naked fetal position at the side of the single bed in his room.

As Willard confronts his memories two servicemen approach the room with orders for Willard to report to General Corman (G.D. Spradlin).

Corman's aide Col. Lucas (Harrison Ford) questions Willard about various episodes in his military career. Willard demurs saying that if the events mentioned did occur he would not be able to comment on them because they were classified.

Corman invites Willard to lunch over which his next mission is revealed. There is a rogue officer, Col. Walter Kurtz (Marlon Brando) who has taken unauthorized command of some guerilla fighters and in the process has executed three agents who were working for the US Army.

The upshot of all the photos, a sound recording of Kurtz and other documentation that Willard peruses is that Corman states that Col. Kurtz has become mentally unbalanced and has to be taken out for the good of the country and the service.

Willard finds that he will be taken to the part of the country where Col. Kurtz can be found in one of the plastic swift boats used to navigate the rivers for inspecting the sampans that resupply the Viet Cong.

As the boat progresses toward a rendezvous with an Air Cavalry unit, Willard looks over the dossier on Col. Kurtz; he is staggered at the man's achievements. Then he questions the decision to eliminate the colonel.

The swift boat sees a squadron of helicopters fly overhead. The choppers attack and destroy a village.

In the midst of the chaos and carnage Willard presents his orders to Lt. Col. Kilgore (Robert Duvall) indicating that the helicopter aircav unit should escort him and the swift boat to the place where they can penetrate the coast and make their way upriver.

Kilgore finds out that one of the crew members on the swift boat is a famous surfer. He tells Lance Johnson (Sam Bottoms) that there are ideal surfing conditions near one of the entry points for the swift boat. When his aides tell him that they have lost one of their men near the village where he intends to deposit Willard, he says "Slopes don't surf."

To prepare the surfing area, Kilgore mounts an all-out attack on the village that puts up some resistance, but ultimately cannot resist the onslaught of the aircav troops.

Even with an after battle cook-out with various brands of beer Willard thinks that Kilgore is not a bad officer, he's just one who has determined different priorities from the usual chain of command.

William Behr Mueller

Willard and the boat depart for their journey upriver. The crew aboard the swift boat ignores Willard as he continues to investigate the background of Col. Kurtz.

The boat comes upon a bizarrely lit stopping point in the river. It's a corrupt dope and supply point that doles out supplies as the duty clerk sees fit. Willard will have none of that and roughs up the clerk telling him to give them fuel.

Later, the crew and a few hundred other GIs watch a USO show with Playmates from Hugh Hefner's empire. The men are excited by the sexual moves of the Playmates and rush the stage causing the helicopter that brought them there to lift off with GIs clinging to the landing sponsons. The GIs ultimately drop into the lagoon.

The next day on the river a sampan is spotted that Chief Philips (Albert Hall), the boat commander wants to investigate telling Willard that until they get to his destination he's just a passenger.

Philips tells Jay Hicks (Frederick Forrest) to board the sampan and check it out. Hicks yells that there is nothing on board except produce.

Lance thinks that Hicks is in jeopardy and he opens fire. The others fire as well, ultimately killing all the people aboard the sampan.

Hicks finds a puppy that caused the firefight.

Philips sees a woman who is still alive. He says they will take her to an ARVN hospital. Willard will not have that interruption so he shoots the wounded woman. Lance cradles the puppy as the others find Willard's behavior incomprehensible.

The boat comes up to a well lit bridge that is in the middle of a firefight. Some survivors swim out to be picked up by the boat but they're ignored. Finally a runner with information from Command for Willard shows up and Willard leaves the boat to cross to the side of the river still controlled by US forces.

Willard and Lance enter a trench with GIs who are either stoned or firing wildly at targets illuminated by star shell. He tries to find out who is in command but finds there is no one to talk to.

Back at the boat, Willard has to drive the boat commander to take him upriver into what is going to be ultimate danger from Philip's point of view.

The next day the mail is distributed as the boat moves through a narrowing channel. Willard finds out that the man previously sent on the same mission has turned coat and become one of Kurtz' aides.

Suddenly the boat comes under attack and one of the crew is killed as the tape from his folks continues to play. And the puppy is nowhere to be found.

Another attack with arrows and Philips is speared and dies, but not before he attempts to kill Willard.

A montage of riverbank destruction greets the boat as Willard tears up all the documentation on Kurtz.

A flotilla of dugouts allows the boat to pass. A photojournalist (Dennis Hopper) introduces himself. He tells Willard that all the men on the shore are Kurtz' "children."

Willard tells Hicks that if he's not back in two hours that he is to call in the airstrike that will annihilate Kurtz and all his troops.

William Behr Mueller

Willard sees Kurtz and they talk. Kurtz asks Willard whether he's an assassin and then tells Willard that he's "an errand boy sent by grocery clerks to collect the bill."

Willard is put into a bamboo cage attended to by the photojournalist. The photojournalist waxes poetic about Kurtz' legacy while Willard smokes a common cigarette.

Kurtz appears in camo makeup and deposits Hicks' head in Willard trussed up lap. There will be no airstrike. Willard is released and fed by Asian women.

Kurtz recounts an anecdote about the epiphany he had when he and his special forces men inoculated a group of children with anti-polio vaccine. Afterwards the enemy came into the village and hacked off the children's arms with the inoculation site. He then uses that insight to carry on his special kind of war.

The ritual slaughter of a bull is shown next coupled with a radio transmission from the base waiting for the order to send airplanes in. Willard has to come to the conclusion that he will kill Kurtz just as Lance is killing the bull. Both are done in with blades.

Outside of the temple complex Willard receives the obeisance of all of Kurtz' "children" as he is now the strongman after killing Kurtz, but he will have none of it as he walks through the crowd on his way back to the boat. He takes Lance by the hand as the troops discard their weapons.

On the boat Willard turns off the radio. He doesn't want an airstrike.

For a glimpse into the Vietnam War, this film gives you a fair picture of the horror and the pointlessness of body counts, riverboat inspections and the priorities of some commanders. Coppola used the Philippines to good advantage to give an impression of what the countryside in Vietnam, Laos and Cambodia is like. The actors in the film show the torment that certain missions provide both when they happen and subsequently. Bring a strong stomach when you decide to watch this film.

William Behr Mueller

Beau Geste

Sand blows over a carved board and exposes the title of the film. The credits in this William Wellman 1939 version of the classic story follow.

A graphic of an Arabian proverb indicates that a brother's love for his brother is much stronger than a man's love for a woman.

A column of French legionnaires rides toward the relief of Fort Zinderneuf. The commander, Major Beaujolais tells the bugler (Robert Preston) to wake the fort's garrison. No movement from the men in the embrasures of the walls.

Beaujolais tells the Bugler to climb the wall and open the gates.

Shortly two rifle shots come from the fort, but neither hits any of the men in the column. Beaujolais says that he will also climb the rope to investigate why the Bugler hasn't opened the gates.

Inside the fort, Beaujolais calls out for the Bugler, but gets no response. He goes up to the firing platform behind the embrasures to see two bodies, one who died peacefully and the other with a French bayonet through his heart. He takes a confession from the man who died from the bayonet wound. He reads that the man has confessed to stealing the sapphire known as "The Blue Water" from Brandon Abbas.

Continuing to investigate, Beaujolais doesn't find the Bugler or any other sign of life. He opens the gate and then an attack by the Tauregs appears to be starting. The column retreats to the oasis. Beaujolais sends two of this troopers for help. As he turns he sees that the fort has erupted in flames.

A flashback takes us to Brandon Abbas fifteen years earlier. The Geste brothers play with ships on a pond. John the youngest of the Gestes receives a bullet wound from one of the cannons on board the model ships.

After Beau has removed the bullet and Gussie says that he will tell Aunt Pat (Heather Thatcher), Major Beaujolais (Henry Stephenson) and Aunt Pat arrive to meet the Gestes, Gussie and Isobel.

After leaving the children, Pat shows Beaujolais a secret place called the Priest's retreat behind the fireplace. She opens a secret compartment and takes "The Blue Water" out and shows it to Beaujolais. It is the last bit of property that the uncle has not gambled away.

A rainy day at Brandon Abbas and the children have to find an inside game. Beau climbs into a suit of armor as King Arthur. The others hide.

Aunt Pat accompanied by a man in a turban comes in and he gives her an envelope. Beau is privy to their conversation, but he doesn't reveal what he knows to the others.

A graphic moves the story forward until the children are adults.

John (Ray Milland) is infatuated with Isabelle. Beau (Gary Cooper) and Digby (Robert Preston) have second thoughts about killing a cute mouse. Gussie is still Gussie.

A telegram arrives telling Aunt Pat that Sir Hector is returning. The others especially Gussie say that Hector never arrives at that time of the year. Aunt Pat says it can only mean he needs money.

William Behr Mueller

Beau asks Aunt Pat to show them The Blue Water since if Hector sells it they won't have a chance to see it again. She brings the jewel into the drawing room and they all marvel at it. Suddenly the lights go off and when they come back on the jewel is gone.

None of the people in the room have stolen the gem (or so it seems). Digby searches Gussie and comes up empty. They all turn in.

John searches the drawing room in the morning, but doesn't find The Blue Water. Digby comes in and shows John a note he's received from Beau who has left Brandon Abbas saying that he took the jewel.

Digby soon follows Beau, leaving John with a note telling him that he, too, is off to the Foreign Legion.

A title tells us that we are at the fort where all the new recruits are housed before their permanent assignment.

John shows up to see that Beau and Digby are already there, in uniform.

After a night of celebration the inebriated men return to the barracks and decide to sleep outside so they can get some rest. While they muse about having stolen the jewel, Rasinoff (J. Carrol Naish) overhears them claim to be jewel thieves.

Later Rasinoff tries to steal the jewel from Beau, but is caught and punished. Sergeant Markoff (Brian Donleavy) finds out from Rasinoff that Beau has the jewel.

The next morning the garrison is given their assignments. Beau and John will go to relieve Fort Zinderneuf and Digby will go to Fort Tokutu for mounted camel training.

At Zinderneuf, Markoff continues to be a martinet, but is chastised by Lt. Dufour (James Burke).

The men have to deal with poor food, death or sickness and the possibility of a Taureg attack. One of the men has a plan to assassinate Markoff if he becomes the commander since Dufour is down with one of the many fevers that occur in the desert.

Dufour dies and Markoff takes command, telling the men that discipline will be severe. He emphasizes that information with his stock phrase "I promise you."

Two deserters are brought back to Zinderneuf, but Markoff will not let them return; instead, he tells his Arab scouts to take them back to the desert and not let them near the oasis.

Schwartz (Albert Dekker) tells the men that it is time for them to mutiny. Beau and John and one other man decide to remain loyal to the flag. Schwartz takes a rifle and tells them that no one leaves the room until they mutiny in the morning. He sends Voisin (Harold Huber) to make sure the guards are with them.

Voisin goes to Markoff and informs him of the planned mutiny. Later Markoff and Rasinoff capture the guards and tell the Gestes to arm themselves. Markoff then wakes the rest of the garrison and tells them the mutiny is over.

Outside, Markoff stands Schwartz and his fellow conspirator against the gate and tells Beau and John to shoot them. They refuse. Just as Markoff is about to kill Beau so that he can get the jewel that Rasinoff told him that Beau has the Tauregs attack.

The mutineers are armed and sent to the walls to fend off the attack. They fire fast and furiously, much to Markoff's delight.

William Behr Mueller

Later, after the men have dressed and eaten, the Tauregs come back for another go at the fort. Many on both sides are killed. Markoff takes the bodies of the fallen soldiers and props them up in the embrasures saying that the next bullet they take won't hurt nearly as much as the first one. Beau and John have survived the attacks.

The Tauregs make a night attack and more of the Legionnaires fall.

Markoff continues to prop the bodies in the embrasures. He sends Rasinoff up to the tower. Rasinoff looks at the Tauregs, but they don't attack.

Markoff says they are listening to their holy men, so he decides that his vastly reduced garrison will sound like they are fully manned. He orders the men to laugh. They do and Rasinoff has such a grotesque giggle that the others laugh even louder.

Rasinoff is shot and the final battle is on. More soldiers fall. Finally Beau is shot.

John tells Markoff that if he touches Beau's body he will kill him.

When John comes back Markoff has rifled through Beau's tunic. John throws the food and drink for Markoff down and takes out his bayonet. Markoff is ready to empty his revolver into John when Beau kicks out and Markoff goes down with John's bayonet in his chest.

John takes food and water and fires the mysterious shots that were heard at the arrival of the relief column from Fort Tokutu. John then abandons the fort.

Digby comes in and sees Beau lying there. Major Beaujolais climbs into the fort as we saw in the beginning and Digby has to hide his bugle and pretend that he is one of the dead Legionnaires.

The rest of the mystery is solved as Digby takes Beau's body and Markoff's body and gives Beau a Viking's funeral. He leaves the fort.

The shots that Beaujolais and the others thought were Tauregs came from John who is reunited with Digby.

Two of the men that Beaujolais sent for reinforcements call for John and Digby. They join forces and head for Egypt. On the way they find an oasis that is crawling with Tauregs. Digby volunteers to go to the top of a dune, blow his bugle and pretend that there are vast numbers of Legionnaires waiting to attack the Tauregs.

One of the fleeing Tauregs shoots Digby.

The scene shifts to Brandon Abbas and Aunt Pat reads the letter that Beau sent explaining what he heard while he was in the suit of armor.

She says that it was a gallant gesture for Beau to have taken the fake Blue Water. Beau Geste, she says was exactly the right name for the man.

This film is one of those that was part of a culmination of excellent acting, good directing and editing and had a story to tell. All the players have departed the scene, but they left a vastly entertaining piece of work that is well worth experiencing.

William Behr Mueller

Big Fish

Do you live in the here and now or are you one who would rather invent your own life? Either way you'll be treated to both ways to get from birth to death in this movie in a series of flashbacks and flash forwards.

Young Ed Bloom (Ewan McGregor) fishes in a river in Alabama to open the film. He narrates his quest for the biggest catfish said to inhabit the waters in which he casts his line. He gets a bite and then hauls in a catfish that's as big as he is.

As Bloom ages he continues to tell his fantastic stories to kids camping and adults and especially to his son. One of the most interesting is when he accepts a dare to visit a witch's house to get her glass eye and take it back to his gang. He meets the witch (Helena Bonham Carter) and she accompanies him back to the rest of the gang and opens her glass eye and shows two of the boys how they will die.

Much later, when the son Will, (Billy Crudup) prepares for his wedding, his wife to be Josephine (Marion Cotillard) is enthralled by his father's tale. Will has heard it so many times he is bored by the retelling.

Later, aboard a river boat on the Seine, a mature Bloom (Albert Finney) regales the audience with the perfect bait for the big fish—his wedding ring. Will confronts his father and asks why he can't grow up and forget about all the stories that he told Will as a child. Bloom says he's sorry for having embarrassed his son.

Living and working in Paris, Will and his wife seem to be a happy couple. Will in the meantime has nothing to do with his father, always making contact with his mother Sandra (Jessica Lange). She realizes that Will talking with his father will only lead to another set of bent feelings so she takes the calls.

One day, however, Sandra has to make a call to Will telling him that his father is doing poorly. Will and Josephine fly back to the US.

Bloom is in bed and Will takes a can of Ensure to get him to take some nourishment. They begin a tentative relationship and Will asks his father to tell him the truth behind all the tall tales.

In Bloom's home town he becomes an athletic hero and opens a highly successful landscaping business. The only fly in his perfect ointment is that a giant has been spotted outside of town and has petrified the townsfolk. Much like his confrontation of the witch, Bloom says that he will go to the giant.

When he sees the giant, bedraggled and covered with leaves, Bloom says he is there to offer himself as a human sacrifice. Karl the giant (Matthew McGrory) refuses to eat Bloom and Bloom tells Karl that the town is too small for both of them.

After cleaning Karl up, Bloom and Karl leave and come to a crossroads. Karl takes one branch and Bloom takes the other. Bloom confronts numerous dangers in the "shortcut" including jumping spiders. He finally comes out to a brilliantly lit village with shoes dangling on wires strung from building to building.

Bloom's encounters in the village named "Spectre" are unusual to say the least. He speaks with Norther Winslow (Steve Buscemi) about the poem Winslow's been working on for ten years. The three lines of the poem make Bloom incredulous and Winslow angry.

William Behr Mueller

At a town party Bloom announces that even though Spectre is a perfect town he's not ready to settle down yet and he leaves. In the forest trees entangle him but let him go when he says that isn't the way he's supposed to die.

He meets Karl who asks where his shoes are. Bloom says they preceded him when actually they became part of the shoe trophies in Spectre.

We come back to Bloom who is at the dinner table telling Josephine about the French speaking natives in the Congo. Will tells his father that Josephine actually went to the Congo for a story. Next Bloom is in bed with Josephine attending. Shortly he recounts the story of exploring the circus and finding the woman he's going to marry. First, however, he has to work in the circus with the understanding that the ringmaster (Danny de Vito) will tell him something of the woman for each month of his employment (without pay).

Finally Bloom finds out her name and where she is going to college.

At her college, Bloom finds out that Sandra Templeton (Alison Lohman) is engaged to the man Bloom beat out in every sport in his home town. After Bloom receives a severe beating Sandra calls the engagement off and Bloom goes to the hospital to recuperate.

While bandaged and splinted Bloom finds out he's been drafted. To shorten the time he will be away from Sandra he volunteers for airborne service and parachutes into the midst of a Chinese USO show in which a Siamese twin performs. Bloom quickly overcomes all the guards.

Concocting an elaborate plan to escape with the twins, Bloom takes months to complete the journey. In the meantime, Sandra receives news of Bloom's death. She is crushed.

Sometime later he shows up and they are reunited.

In bed Will and Josephine talk about his father and she says that he's never told her exactly how his parents came together. He tells her that what his father has told him doesn't make sense.

With Bloom in bed enjoying a late breakfast, Will asks his mother for time to speak with his father. She and Josephine leave.

Will confronts his father about the stories and asks his father to be who he really is. Blood tells Will that he's always been who he is and if his son can't see that then it's the son's fault not his.

Outside Will cleans the pond and is surprised by a big fish. Shortly he gives up on the pond and he and his mother and Josephine explore the garage where fishing lures and memorabilia galore reside. Will finds some proof of his father's exploits.

After the war Bloom finds a job as a traveling salesman. He becomes so proficient at the job that his territory expands as does the merchandize he purveys.

About to make a deposit in a bank he meets Norther Winslow from Spectre, a real surprise in Texas. He finds out that Norther is about to rob the savings and loan. Norther invites Bloom to help him rob the bank.

Later after Bloom has found out that the savings and loan is bankrupt he gives Norther the money he was going to deposit.

William Behr Mueller

Norther says that he needs to go to Wall Street because that's where the real money is.

Sometime after Norther has become rich he sends ten thousand to Bloom who buys his wife a real house with a white picket fence.

Bloom appears to be suicidal as we see him submerged in a bathtub. He makes a comedic excuse to his wife who joins him in the tub.

As Bloom and his wife soak in the tub, Will finds a deed of trust made out to Jennifer Hill. He drives to Spectre and confronts Jennifer about exactly how she and his father came to make out the deed.

Turns out that Bloom experienced a fantastic rain storm leaving his car high in a tree. He finds his way back to Spectre and finds it dilapidated because of a new highway that bypassed the town.

Because he wants to see the town survive, he goes back to all his acquaintances and gets them to contribute to a trust that will own the town.

The last person to sell their property to the trust is Jennifer Hill (Helena Bonham Carter). She lives in the same house that young Bloom on the dare confronted the witch. Now the house is even more run down. She refuses to sell.

Bloom enlists the help of Karl to push the house back to a plumb position and then as the months pass he completely rehabs the house until it looks newer than new.

Jennifer has fallen in love with Bloom but he tells her that he will love his wife and only his wife for the rest of his days.

Will returns to the house to find his father and family gone.

At the hospital, Bloom is comatose. Will volunteers to stay with him and when Bloom regains semi-consciousness Will becomes the storyteller.

As in Will's story, all the people from Bloom's life attend the funeral and Will comes to the conclusion that if you hear a story enough times the storyteller becomes the story.

Be prepared for at least one hankie at the end of this film. Two if you are on the edge of emotion. The stories in the film are the stuff of legend and you will probably have a hard time remembering all of Bloom's adventures, but that's a good reason to watch the film again.

Brassed Off

If there is any origin to be pinpointed for this movie it would have to be the reign of Margaret Thatcher as Prime Minister. She belonged to the conservative party, AKA "Tories" and they were the politicians most closely aligned with business. In this case, the business of mining coal.

Most English speakers probably have little or no idea what "Brassed Off" means, so explanatory titles introduce the film to provide the viewer with background on some of the British colloquialisms.

Seeing the miners at work in the dirty sweaty underground pit follows as the opening credits display. Then they walk toward their dressing room where they can shower off the coal dust and get ready to go home.

Other scenes in the town of Grimley show that wives and others are fighting against closing the coal mine.

A young woman, Gloria (Tara Fitzgerald) arrives and takes a room. She has to convince the landlady that she will not be practicing her Flugelhorn within the room. The landlady says that she should go over to where the local band is practicing.

We cut to a bar with Andy (Ewan McGregor) losing money he's earned at the mine at pool.

Next, two wives Vera (Sue Johnston) and Ida (Mary Healey) mention that the band is going to dissolve as their last practice is that evening.

Danny (Pete Postlethwaite) the band's conductor and chief money raiser leaves his dwelling riding a bicycle dressed in his band uniform (with music provided by the Grimthorpe Colliery Band). He is on his way to the band's last practice.

Vera's and Ida's husbands Jim (Philip Jackson) and Ernie (Peter Martin) leave with their instruments and the admonition to make sure that it's the last time they will be giving up money to support the band. They hone their response to Danny's request for support money.

In Gloria's room the TV drones on about the Grimley mine closing as Gloria fondles her Flugel.

In the bar, Andy watches the same TV presentation that Gloria is hearing. He still loses at pool.

Danny's son Phil (Stephen Tompkinson) and his wife Sandra (Melanie Hill) talk about the offer the mine owners have made before he is off to practice with the band. As Phil leaves she throws a plate at him and Danny, who says "Sandra's a bit clumsy with the crockery."

Harry (Jim Carter[butler on Downtown Abbey]) leaves as Danny and Phil pedal off humming one of their band's tunes. His wife mislabels his horn as a trumpet and he says "It's a euphonium."

Their humming dissolves into the band playing the same piece at the practice hall. Phil's old trombone can't quite make the grade, making Danny shake his head.

Danny's comment on the piece was "A load of crap. That's what it was a load of bloody crap." He is brought up short by Harry who asks him whether he's been on holiday since "Pit's under threat." Danny will have none of that economic talk, not when there's music to be played and played rightly. "It's music that matters."

Jim attempts to put Danny off on their contribution when Gloria walks in. Danny thinks she's off the beaten path while the others consider her female attributes. She finally tell them that she's a native of Grimley and Danny explains that her granddad has his picture on the wall of honor for the Grimley band.

She's invited to play with the band saying that she's been practicing Rodrigo's *Concierto de Aranjuez*, "Orange Juice to you," Danny says by way of explanation. Andy renews his acquaintance with Gloria who says she's been doing "this and that." Then we are treated to a band version of the piece and the band members are blown away with her playing.

While the band makes such glorious music, the negotiating session between the owners and the miners is intercut with the music.

After the end Danny says "And she calls that wobbly." They applaud her performance. Afterwards Danny appears to be ill, coughing into a handkerchief.

The scene shifts to the union hall where there is much debate about the redundancy offer that is being made by the owners. Phil is adamantly opposed.

At home, Phil and Sandra continue their argument about money. And then the loan collectors show up and badger him for repayment.

Danny and the band are off to a band competition, but they lose to all the other bands. The only consolation is beer, and plenty of it.

Back at the practice hall, Jim tells Danny they'll play while the pit's open, but the moment it closes they'll pack it in. Danny is crushed.

While Andy and Gloria are off to get some "grub," Phil finds out that Danny is not physically fit.

Gloria has to admit that she works for the mine owners and that revelation means that Andy's notion of getting together with Gloria appears to be shattered. She tries to get him to understand that she is on their side and that her report will show that the mine is profitable and shouldn't be closed. Outside she offers coffee, he says he doesn't drink coffee to which she replies that she hasn't got any.

Later Phil contemplates breaking into the shop that has a new trombone. He's talked out of it by other band members.

The next morning Danny sees Andy coming out of Gloria's rooms. The miners vote on redundancy and then it's back to the pit (with colliery band music to move things along).

Gloria confronts the CEO of the owners and pleads with him about her report and closing the mine. He gives the impression that her report is exactly what is needed to keep the mine open.

Outside the band members see Gloria emerge from the owner's building. Once again she's on their shit list, making it hard for Andy to think about a continuing relationship.

Inside the bar, Jim has some harsh words for Andy and his relationship with Gloria.

Then it's time for Phil's "Mr. Chuckles." Phil has to earn some money to pay for the new trombone. He's an inept clown and it's tough for Sandra to pay for groceries on the money she gets from him. He comes home to find the collection agents taking things out of his house. He prevails on them to give him more time to come up with the repayment.

With high hopes the band is off to another contest. Phil has a new trombone that is the last straw for Sandra. And it's also the last gasp of the men who hope the mine will remain open. The collection agents return to Phil and Sandra's place and repossess all the furniture.

The nadir of the mining community is partially offset by the band winning the semi-final competition. Back in Grimley the band faces the reality of the mine closing. Danny's health finally gives out and he is hospitalized. Sandra takes the kids and leaves Phil with an empty house and his father in the hospital.

In a rare tribute the band with miner's headlamps stand outside Danny's hospital window and play a heartfelt rendition of "Danny Boy." At the end of the performance they present Danny with a new baton (instead of flowers).

Gloria confronts the mine owners with her assessment of when the decision was made to close the mine. Rather than the few months of negotiations they decided two years ago to close it. She is incensed and quits her job. She and Andy make up while Phil is hesitant about telling Danny that the band is going to pack it in now that the mine has closed.

Mr. Chuckles goes berserk at a party and Phil attempts suicide. In the hospital he confronts Danny about what matters in life: music.

As the band members have a beer, Gloria shows up with a new bank account in the band's name. It's enough money for them to go to the final contest in London at the Albert Hall.

In the immense crowd in Albert Hall, the band strikes up the familiar coda of The William Tell Overture. Their performance is superb and they win the trophy, but Danny comes out and says that they are going to refuse it so they will have some attention paid to them as he explains all the trials and tribulations that the miners have gone through.

After Jim tells the emcee that they are going to take the trophy they get on a London double decker and play "Pomp and Circumstance."

This film may well be a "message" film but it rises above that characterization to provide excellent brass band music, good acting and an emotional trip through the English heartland. Enjoy.

Breaker Morant

The Boer War or as the Brits named it "The Anglo Boer War" was a three-year long attempt to conquer what would be termed "freedom fighters" today. From 1898 to 1901 the British Army went from defeat to victory over the ragtag elements of the farmer army that faced them with the most modern weapons available at the time. The film begins with a title that gives a brief explanation of what the Boer War was all about.

To set the scene a small army band on a gazebo strikes up the military march "Soldiers of the Queen" as citizens of Pietersburg are shown.

Pietersburg is the place where three of the Bushveldt Carabineers are incarcerated awaiting adjudication of their alleged crime of murdering captured Boer prisoners and a German missionary.

In the stark hall where the preliminary investigation has taken place, one of the presiding officers asks the three prisoners: Lt. Harry "Breaker" Morant (Edward Woodward), Lt. Peter Handcock (Bryan Brown) and Lt. George Ramsdale Witton (Lewis Fitz-Gerald) whether they have anything to add to the notes on the inquiry.

Morant stands and provides a brief bio of what he'd done since coming to South Africa.

After the statement the scene shifts to Pretoria and Lord Kitchener's headquarters where Maj. Charles Bolton (Rod Mullinar) who will be the prosecutor for the three accused reports to get the brief for the trial. He is told that it will be an open and shut case since the defense will be provided by one of the Australian officers, Maj. J.F. Thomas (Jack Thompson).

The accused meet Maj. Thomas who admits that this will be his first court martial and that he was only a country solicitor handling land conveyances and wills. That revelation prompts a retort from Handcock that his experience in that area might be handy.

To see how the accusations came about the scene shifts to a patrol about to attack a farmhouse that has been said to contain only a few worn-out Boer fighters with spent horses. Captain Hunt (Terence Donovan) poo-poohs a negative assessment by his translator and guide Christiaan Botha (Russell Kiefel) that the scene is too quiet. Hunt takes all but three men forward to attempt to either capture or kill the Boers in the farmhouse. They are surprised and many are killed. Hunt is wounded and waits for the Boer leader to emerge when he shoots him.

When the remnant of the patrol returns to Fort Edward, Morant immediately confronts Captain Taylor (John Waters) about his shoddy intelligence. Taylor tells him to "avenge Captain Hunt."

At the farmhouse, Morant sees that Hunt's body has been mutilated. That infuriates Morant who leads his group after the Boers who disfigured Hunt.

After they rout the Boers, one of them is found hiding in a wagon. He is wearing Captain Hunt's jacket. Morant's fury demands that he be executed immediately, giving rise to the charge that there was a conspiracy among the officers to murder the Boer prisoner.

William Behr Mueller

At the court martial, Maj. Thomas rises to the occasion forcing one prosecution witness after another to either recant or admit that what was considered normal army behavior had to be modified to be able to fight the Boer on his own terms.

The presiding officer at the trial Lt. Col. Denny (Charles Tingwell) demands that Morant provide some explanation as to the rule under which the Boer prisoner was shot. Morant strides to the front of the room and tells Denny and the other officers that they didn't have rulebooks in the field, that their focus was on killing as many of the Boers as possible and that the prisoner was executed under rule "303," the marking stamped on the receiver of their rifles.

That night Morant is prevailed upon to read one of the poems he's working on. When the men retire they dream of home and we see some of the background that has motivated them to fight in South Africa.

The next day a Boer attack on the gaol and the garrison means that the prisoners are given arms and help to drive off the Boer group.

Maj. Thomas attempts to use the reaction of the prisoners in helping to fight off the Boer attack as justification, based on the Duke of Wellington's admonition that men who show courage even after having been accused of wrongdoing should be pardoned. Lt. Col. Denny says that the Duke's words have no applicability in the current case.

To get to the nut of the order to take no Boer prisoners, Maj. Thomas requests that Lord Kitchener attend the court martial.

Kitchener avoids going to the trial and instead sends Col. Hamilton who says that he cannot recall having a conversation with Captain Hunt on anything related to military matters in the Transvaal.

Later, Maj. Thomas confides in the three that even though there appears to be some sympathy among members of the court the outcome will hinge on how they view the shooting of the Rev. Hess. He also has a dim view of Handcock's story of what he was doing instead of shooting Hess.

Maj. Thomas finds out that the corporal who testifies about how Handcock went after Hess has a grudge against Handcock and is willing to carry it out at the trial.

After a stirring final speech in which Maj. Thomas sets forth the differences between normal men who go to war and behave in abnormal circumstances compared to abnormal men who go to war and behave as they always have, the men wait to find out their fates.

Maj. Thomas brings champagne to the men and tells them that two of the judges voted for acquittal, but Captain Taylor tells Morant not to be too sure of the final verdict. He also says that he will provide a horse, but Morant says that it's not for him.

The verdict is death for Morant and Handcock and life imprisonment for Witton. Morant refuses a chaplain stating that he is a Pagan. Handcock agrees. Morant asks for an epitaph that the chaplain reads: "And a man's foes *shall be* they of his own household."

William Behr Mueller

The end of the film is poignant and there are titles to tell the viewer what happened to those men after they left South Africa.

Edward Woodward sings the lyrics to "Soldiers of the Queen" as the explanatory titles are displayed.

Watching this film you can see that Bruce Beresford, the Director, took a powerful stage play and made an equally powerful movie with a great cast, sparkling dialog and a view of how military minds operate when it comes to the sacrifice of some of their own.

Cold Comfort Farm

Aunt Ada Doom (Sheila Burrell) as a child begins the film crossing through a thicket to approach a wood shed where she sees "something nasty." Thus begins a lifelong recitation that provides Aunt Ada with the power over the rest of the Starkadder clan to weld them to Cold Comfort Farm because "There's always been Starkadders on Cold Comfort Farm."

A relatively poor long-lost relative known only as Robert Poste's child by the Starkadders, but who does have a name Flora Poste (Kate Beckinsale) arrives at her friend Mrs. Smiley's (Joanna Lumley) home in London. She has aspirations of becoming a writer in the vein of Jane Austen and wants to visit some of her relatives to experience the sort of life that Jane cataloged in her books. She tells her friend that she has a compunction to organize and tidy up so she should be able to survive anything she might find in the countryside.

To that end, Flora writes to her relatives and receives replies, most of which are negative. However, she receives a handwritten note from Judith Starkadder (Eileen Atkins) telling her that she will be most welcome at Cold Comfort Farm.

On the farm Judith in her ultra gloomy fashion breaks the news to the rest of the clan that Robert Poste's Child is coming to stay. The rest of the clan react negatively since they think that Flora has some designs on the farm and that their tenancy might be limited or eliminated.

Taking the train and trying to puzzle out a meaning and application for the "golden orb" in her notes Flora arrives at the station where she has to wake Adam Lambsbreath (Freddie Jones) on his manure stained trap.

After traveling some distance Flora sees the farm, a more than somewhat dilapidated collection of buildings with nothing to recommend them as a suitable place for a well dressed and coifed young woman to reside.

She enters to find the interior of the house even more disorganized and the clan somewhat hostile. Judith takes her upstairs to a room that doesn't appear to have been lived in for many years. That will never do and Flora indicates some of the changes she requires, most of which are seen as unnecessary by Judith.

Organizing and tidying up, Flora gets a new whisk brush for Adam who has been cleaning the porridge bowls with a stick. She also convenes afternoon tea with suspicious Reuben and Seth thinking that once again Robert Poste's child has ulterior motives.

Not content with moving the Starkadders to a more comfortable and genteel way of life, she works on Aunt Ada, who ultimately allows Flora to come into her room, much to the amazement of some of the others who live at Cold Comfort Farm.

Reuben still thinks that Flora has designs on the farm and she finally convinces him that such is not the case.

There's still the problem of Elfine who emulates a wood sprite in flowing green chiffon. Flora chances upon a meeting between the young lord of the nearby manor and Elfine and Flora decides that Elfine needs to go after him.

In London at her friend's various haberdashers, Elfine is fitted out with a sumptuous ball gown and afterwards goes to a party at which she is told that what they are doing is not "such fun" but merely diverting.

Seth drives Flora and Elfine to the 21st birthday bash for the young lord and Elfine dazzles the attendees. At the end the young lord announces that he and Elfine are engaged.

In the meantime, Aunt Ada senses that some people are missing and she calls for "The Counting," which usually occurs twice a year. The partygoers arrive just in time to be included.

Seth is a problem since he is a movie buff, but Flora has already seen the film that he is eager to see. All is not lost as a movie producer who is an acquaintance of Flora's shows up at the farm. Once he sees Seth's potential screen presence he convinces Seth to accompany him back to Hollywood. Judith is heartbroken that her son is leaving Cold Comfort Farm.

More work for Flora as she hooks up Reuben with one of the farm women.

Only Aunt Ada Doom, Adam and Amos Starkadder (Ian McKellen) require Flora's organization and tidying up.

She accompanies Amos to his church where he literally preaches hell fire and tells the congregation that they will all burn, suitable forewarned by reminding them how it felt to have a finger burned on a stove. Flora cannot stand the sermon and leaves to go to a tea room for refreshment.

Mybug (Stephen Fry) is an erstwhile writer who thinks he's madly in love with Flora. He sees her in the tea shop. She wishes that he would leave. Amos sees her, enters the shop and drags Flora away from the clutches of Mybug.

On the way back to the farm, Flora tells Amos that he should preach to the multitudes and he could with a small van. He appears to warm to the idea.

Back at the farm, Amos tells Judith that he's felt the calling and will be off in his minivan to preach to the wide world. Judith feels another flight of slings and arrows as now her husband is leaving.

Flora's tidying up of Elfine is only partially completed and will finally result in the be all and end all of a woman's fate at the time: marriage.

Flora finally convinces Aunt Ada to shrug off her weeds and stringy hair and enjoy life. A very ornate party for all the country folk and the manor people swings into a lively tempo. Aunt Ada makes a speech that shows the assembled guests that she is no longer the frump they have come to expect. In fact she is off to Paris.

Flora is still trying to resolve the issue of the "golden orb" when her love flies a biplane around the farm and lands in a field. She runs over to him and they fly away to live happily ever after.

The film ends with Adam leading his prize cows to the manor house, leaving Cold Comfort Farm with the blessing of Aunt Ada.

With good thirties music, wonderful sets and a cast that fits their roles like the proverbial glove, this film will provide some chuckles and maybe even a guffaw for those who are not too sophisticated to see the humor in a Midlands farm in the period between world wars. You'll probably want to watch it more than once and that will be the best takeaway from all the effort that went into the making of Cold Comfort Farm.

William Behr Mueller

Das Boot

This film will appeal to someone who wants to experience a U-boat war patrol with all the pre-patrol activities, wild weather and vicious counterattacks the men of the U-boat service lived through (that is the quarter of the men who served and returned alive).

As the film opens naval personnel drive in a small car along a dirt road. They are accosted by some other very drunk naval personnel. The driver is *Kapitan-leutnant* Willenbrock (Jurgen Prochnow). Willenbrock identifies the drunken sailors as part of his crew before they have to report for another patrol.

Willenbrock and his companions make it to a cabaret that is in full party mood. Some of his officers are as drunk as the ratings who tried to stop the car.

Willenbrock introduces a Correspondent (Herbert Gronemeyer) and then the uproar gets even louder because the U-boat men are celebrating the victory and medals of another U-boat captain, Thomsen who starts to berate Hitler but then turns his venom on Churchill and the crowd laughs at his characterization of the British leader.

The next day Willenbrock goes to the sub pen to take command of his boat. The crew, dressed in their leathers, awaits the captain and his greeting.

Once Willenbrock has made his remarks to the crew they prepare to get underway.

As the U-boat leaves the harbor all the men who can crowd the after space on the bridge (the "Wintergarden") wave to people on the shore.

The Correspondent is very enthusiastic about being on the U-boat and takes roll after roll of film showing the crew and their work places. He is assigned a bunk in the chief's section.

The officer of the first watch (Hubertus Bengsch) is a meticulous eater and the other officers watch him as he dissects his food preparatory to consuming it. He is from Mexico where he worked on a relative's farm.

Willenbrock wants to find out how well his new crew is prepared to evade a surface attack by an allied destroyer. He orders an "alarm" and the crew runs and dives to the front of the boat to assist it in getting under water faster. After the boat has reached a safe depth, Willenbrock tells them that it was a practice dive. They are relieved that there will be no depth charges to follow.

The weather makes up and the boat crashes through very rough seas. The men on bridge watch dive for cover when a breaker smashes over the front of the conning tower. When the helmsman tells Willenbrock that he is having a hard time keeping the boat on course, the captain relents and dives the boat.

Coming up for air as well as to charge the batteries, the boat once again has to fight its way through rough seas. Again Willenbrock dives the boat to give the men some relief. In the forward torpedo room the Correspondent has an oil-soaked rag thrown in his face. No one takes responsibility.

William Behr Mueller

On looking through the periscope the captain sees a destroyer bearing down on them. He takes the boat deeper. The destroyer finds their depth and begins a systematic depth charging, rattling all the men in the boat and causing some damage. Willenbrock takes the boat even deeper and finally the sound of the destroyer in the hydrophone diminishes and everybody is relieved that they don't have to undergo another round of explosions.

Willenbrock receives a radiogram that tells him that there is a convoy within striking distance. He surfaces the boat and looks at the moon. He doesn't like the fact that the sub will be exposed and that the convoy is partially shrouded in fog. None of the other officers see any destroyers accompanying the convoy.

Willenbrock makes a surface attack. Then a destroyer heads directly for them.

As the crew waits for the impact of the torpedoes, the destroyer bears down on the U-boat. The first torpedo explodes, and then the second and finally the third sending ships to the bottom.

Then the destroyer seeks revenge and a vicious depth charging ensues. Willenbrock maneuvers his boat to escape the destroyer and the crew feels relief.

Their happiness and relief is short-lived as a second destroyer joins the attack. The situation aboard the boat becomes hellish.

In the midst of the attack, Johann the chief engineer (Erwin Leder) leaves his battle station and with a mask of intense fear makes his way to the ladder that goes up to the conning tower. Willenbrock orders him back to his station, but his state of fear is so great he does not comply. Willenbrock goes to his quarters and gets a pistol. The others in the control room subdue Johann and stuff him back through the bulkhead hatch before the captain can return. They tell him that Johann is back with his diesel engines.

After many hours of silent running the U-boat escapes the relentless depth charging. Willenbrock sees the intense fire from a tanker through the periscope. It is the same one they torpedoed before the depth charge attack.

The boat surfaces and the captain orders another torpedo launched against the tanker. It explodes. The U-boat officers and the Correspondent see men still aboard the tanker. Willenbrock rhetorically shouts why weren't they rescued after so long a time. The others identify with the men jumping from the tanker, some of whom are ablaze.

Willenbrock orders the boat to back away. He so states in his log.

Johann approaches the captain to make an apology for his behavior. Willenbrock lists the infractions that Johann committed. Johann is fearful that he will have to undergo a court martial. Willenbrock takes pity on Johann because this is his 9th patrol.

A radiogram that is triple coded for the captain's eyes only tells them that they will not return to La Rochelle; rather they will proceed to the base at La Specia after they have refueled and reprovisioned at Vigo on the northwestern tip of Spain. This news is badly received since some of the crew know that for the submarine to reach La Specia it must transit the narrows opposite the Rock of Gibraltar, a place that teems with British ships.

The Correspondent and the chief engineer (Klaus Wennemann) will leave the boat there. The Correspondent takes letters written by one of the crew members to his pregnant French girlfriend.

The boat creeps into Vigo looking for a ship named *Weser*, interned by the Spanish but having fuel and munitions for Willenbrock's boat.

Ashore in the sumptuous dining room, the first watch officer is mistaken by the captain of the *Weser* and he has to apologize to Willenbrock.

The crew is feted as the captain seeks to get a better grasp of what it was like in a submarine.

Naval attache's appear with orders for Willenbrock. They bring bad news. The chief and Correspondent will not leave the ship after all.

The orders are for the U-boat to breach Gibraltar's defenses. It is a fatal order with the narrowness of the Strait of Gibraltar (7 miles) and the numerous ships guarding the strait.

Willenbrock spins a tale of how they will approach the narrows, dive and allow the current to take the U-boat into the Mediterranean.

Moving toward the strait, things appear to be going well, but an aircraft appears and wounds the navigator leaving Willenbrock on the bridge. He orders the submarine to go faster, but the speed is too much for the diesel engines and one starts to come off the plates.

There is nothing for it but to dive because the English ships are firing and hitting the U-boat.

The diving plane is bent and cannot be moved. Willenbrock orders the tanks to be blown to stop the descent of the U-boat, but to no avail. The submarine continues its downward plunge until the depth gauge hits a blank spot beyond the red zone. Then the U-boat finally hits the bottom.

With the increased pressure at that depth (280 meters) the joints cannot hold and water starts to flood the ship. All hands turn to, but there is so many leaks and so little time. Tools are misplaced and shouting finally gets the tools to where they're needed.

Organized chaos reigns supreme. Willenbrock wants proper damage reports, but there is so much to do that there is no time for such.

All the men work themselves into total fatigue, baling water from the aft section and emptying it into the control room bilge.

After 15 hours the Chief Engineer reports to the captain that all the major damage has been repaired.

With immense hope and great expectations the last of the air blows the ballast tanks. A brief surge of the ship and finally the depth gauge starts to reverse and the ship starts to rise.

On the surface, Willenbrock gives the order to start the diesel engines and they do start.

William Behr Mueller

The ship plunges through very rough seas to return to its home port.

Various high ranking officers greet the ship, but then a final ironic twist as a bombing raid kills or wounds most of the crew including Willenbrock who watches the submarine sink in the slot before it was taken into the safety of the fortress. The Correspondent goes to Willenbrock as he dies.

Not a happy ending, but a realistic one. Even though luck appeared to be with Willenbrock and his crew it ultimately ran out as it did for thirty thousand of the forty thousand men who went to sea in German U-boats in World War II.

Dr. Strangelove

Since this film was released during the height of the Cold War there are disclaimers before the credits begin to tell the viewer that the Air Force indicated that none of the cinematic elements shown has any relationship to Air Force protocol.

The credits roll with sky views in the background.

Most of the actors play their roles in comic opera fashion and now they can be seen for the black comedians they saw themselves as during the making of the film with its potentially catastrophic results. Peter Sellers takes on three roles and does an excellent job as Group Captain Lionel Mandrake, President Merkin Muffley and Dr. Strangelove (the ex-Nazi with a strangely behaving right arm).

The film unfolds with Gen. Jack Ripper (Sterling Hayden) telling Mandrake to put Burpelson AFB on full alert, confiscate all radios and send a special code to the B-52 bombers at their fail-safe positions. As Mandrake is shutting down the computers he finds a transistor radio and turns it on to find that there is no attack on the US taking place. He immediately goes to Ripper's office and confronts him with the radio broadcast.

As Ripper and Mandrake spar over the need for an attack on the Soviet Union, Gen. Buck Turgeson (George C. Scott) has his one or more nighters with his secretary interrupted with the news that Ripper has sent the attack code to the aircraft armed with Hydrogen bombs. He has to leave the cozy environment to attend a meeting with the president.

William Behr Mueller

President Muffley and all his aides sit around an enormous table in the War Room. Muffley asks Turgeson to explain why the attack code has been sent to the aircraft.

On board the lead B-52 the radio operator receives the attack code on the plane's special computer. He tells Major Kong (Slim Pickens) that they have been ordered to instigate Plan R. Pickens leaves the cockpit to confirm the communication.

Muffley still cannot get a reason why the aircraft have been ordered to attack the USSR. He calls the Russian Ambassador Alexi de Sadesky (Peter Bull) into the War Room. Turgeson is apoplectic that a "Russki" would be admitted to the confidential confines of the War Room.

On board the B-52 the individual duties in Plan R are distributed by Kong.

Turgeson tussles with Sadesky under the guise that he is taking pictures of the War Room with a spy camera. Muffley is upset that the ambassador would do such a thing.

As the B-52 flies toward its primary target, Kong opens the emergency supply kit and reads the contents to the crew. Sharp eyes will notice that the word "Dallas" has been replaced with "Vegas" to eliminate any reference to JFK's assassination.

Muffley phones Dmitri (Gorbachev's analog) to try to smooth things over about the mistaken attack in progress. When little results from their conversation, Muffley asks one of the other generals in attendance whether Burpelson can be successfully attacked so that he can speak directly to Gen. Ripper.

Aboard the B-52 all the aspects of Plan R are initiated according to the checklist.

Ripper has locked the doors to his office so Mandrake cannot leave to recall the aircraft on his own initiative.

Outside the AFB other troops approach and engage the defenders. Shortly they start to shoot up the building that Ripper and Mandrake are in. Ripper continues with his fantasy that the Commies are behind the evil scheme of fluoridating drinking water and thereby polluting the precious essence of humanity.

Muffley finds out through Sadesky that the Soviets have built a doomsday machine that will cause all life on earth to die off. Muffley asks whether the device can be shut down. Sadesky tells that there is no way.

Dr. Strangelove finds that such a device is very interesting and explains why it cannot be turned off.

Muffley tells Dmitri that he has to shoot down the aircraft that have penetrated his airspace so that the doomsday machine will not detonate.

Ripper commits suicide and Mandrake has to try to determine the correct code for recalling the aircraft.

Aboard Kong's aircraft a missile tracks the plane and finally explodes causing significant damage including destroying the special computer that will receive any recall message.

Col. Bat Guano (Keenan Wynn) confronts Mandrake and they finally get enough coins from a Coke machine so that Mandrake can phone the president with his interpretation of the recall code.

William Behr Mueller

On the situation board most of the aircraft receive the code, but Kong's aircraft does not. Not only is the computer damaged but fuel is leaking.

As Kong's aircraft skims along the surface, another target has to be acquired.

Muffley convinced Dmitri to concentrate his air defenses around the two targets of the B-52 that wasn't shot down. Muffley thinks that is the only way to prevent the doomsday device from exploding.

Kong goes into the bomb bay to fix the mechanism that opens the bomb bay doors while his co-pilot flies the plane to the ICBM missile complex.

Just as Kong gets the doors to open while he is straddling one of the hydrogen bombs the bomb is released and he rides it down to the ultimate way to exit life.

The film ends with one nuclear explosion after another as Vera Lynn sings "We'll meet again, don't know where, don't know when..."

The emotional impact of the film no longer makes audiences leave with a profound depression that such an outcome could actually happen.

If you're a Stanley Kubrick fan you'll enjoy his dark view of what could have happened, but didn't.

Full Metal Jacket

Stanley Kubrick shifted from the black humor of "Doctor Strangelove..." to gritty reality with this film.

Boot camp with a motley crew that Gunny Sergeant Hartman ([R.] Lee Ermey) hopes to bully, berate and, in one case, humiliate into becoming killer Marines.

Every aspect of boot camp life is lovingly chronicled in showing the viewer exactly how civilians are converted from the individuals they were as civilians (first by having all their long hair roughly clipped off) to efficient killing machines.

Hartman is merciless as he assigns nicknames to his platoon. "Joker" (Matthew Modine), "Animal Mother" (Adam Baldwin) and "Gomer Pyle" (Vincent D'Onofrio) are examples of what Hartman considers appropriate appellations for some of his charges.

Bed checks, close order drill and a litany of what a rifle means to a man are all part of the conversion process. Most of the men can run through the obstacle courses, but Pyle cannot do any of them, in fact he cannot even pull himself up once on the chinning bar.

Hartman makes Joker Pyle's mentor and it appears as though with the tender and specialized attention from Joker that Pyle will be able to shape up.

On the rifle range, Hartman is surprised that Pyle is very adept with putting a bullet on the target.

William Behr Mueller

One night Joker is the "night watchman" for the barracks and he hears a strange noise coming from the end of the barracks. He investigates and finds Pyle sitting on one of the toilets in the "head" cradling his rifle. He tells Pyle that if they are discovered it will be even worse than the first time that Pyle screwed up and was pummeled by the rest of the platoon. Pyle continues loading live rounds into his rifle. Joker finds the scene to be disturbing and continually attempts to get Pyle to cease and desist.

Hartman bursts into the head and stridently tells Pyle to put his weapon down. Pyle gets a diabolical look on his face as Joker tells Hartman that Pyle has live rounds in his weapon. Hartman reiterates his command to put the weapon down. Pyle has the weapon pointed at Hartman and then pulls the trigger killing Hartman.

Joker is immobilized with shock and fear.

Pyle puts the gun muzzle into his mouth and pulls the trigger.

The platoon gets its assignments and Hartman is surprised that Joker is going to be part of the public relations unit in Vietnam. Others are assigned to rifle units.

In Vietnam, Joker finds that his assignment is not fulfilling. And he wears a peace button on his uniform, a particularly offensive symbol to the officer in charge.

Joker and his combat photographer find themselves in Da Nang under fire from the North Vietnamese army. The attack appears to be a feint but it does give Joker the itch to get into "real" combat.

The Tet offensive begins and Joker with his photographer go to the city of Hue to document the fighting going on there. He is exposed to the instantaneous death and hidden menace of snipers.

In the squad that Joker is documenting there is an argument about whether to retrieve one of the men who has been shot by the sniper. "Cowboy" is overruled by "Animal Mother" and they advance toward the sniper position. More of the men are shot by the sniper until Mother takes command and they move toward the sniper's position.

Inside the building Joker comes face to face with the sniper, a female, but his gun jams and he takes refuge from the murderous fire coming from the sniper's AK-47. Finally, one of the other men in the squad comes in and cuts the sniper down.

The men of the squad stand over the sniper who is mortally wounded. They want to leave her but Joker says they can't leave her. Mother tells Joker that he's permitted to finish her. He removes his pistol and gives the coup de grace to the sniper.

The squad leave Hue with Joker in a voice over saying how good it feels to be alive.

This movie will give you a gut churning taste of boot camp, different aspects of Marine life and an interesting look back at the war in Vietnam. It's hard to label the movie as "entertaining," but it is an interesting look at what it takes to become a Marine and would be appropriate viewing for anyone opting to join the Corps.

William Behr Mueller

F/X

A rainy night in New York City. A shadowy figure in a trench coat exits a cab and enters a building that is an upscale restaurant. He pulls out a machine gun and proceeds to kill everybody. A very attractive blond pleads for her life—to no avail.

Then the camera pulls back and we see that the scene with all the carnage and destruction is really a movie set. The special effects man Rollie Tyler (Brian Brown) is pleased with all the havoc he's captured on film.

A man enters the set and introduces himself as a producer. Martin Lipton (Cliff De Young) tells Tyler that he has a project he'd like to discuss with him. Early the next morning is agreed on for a meeting.

Tyler's girlfriend, Ellen Keith (Diane Venora) tries to get Tyler to get out of bed for his appointment. She has to leave for an audition.

Lipton shows up and Tyler in his shorts opens the window and throws the key down to Lipton.

When Lipton enters he is shocked by a monster that appears lifelike and moves toward him. Tyler explains that he likes to welcome his guests.

Lipton sees all of the props that Tyler has used in making films come to life. Then he explains what he has in mind—a staged assassination of a mobster that is going into the Witness Protection and Relocation program (WPR). Tyler says he wants to meet Lipton's boss.

In the boss' office Tyler meets Col. Mason (Mason Adams) who gives Tyler more detail about the project. Tyler demurs because of getting a notorious mobster off, but then asks to have 24-hours to think it over.

When Tyler agrees another twist is thrown in—Mason wants Tyler to be the trigger man.

To be able to simulate the assassination Tyler has to make prostheses that will allow him to shoot fake bullets at Nicolas De Franco (Jerry Orbach) and have blood appear on his suit.

After De Franco is prepared he sits at a restaurant that looks eerily similar to the movie set we first saw. Tyler with a fake moustache nervously waits outside the restaurant and then enters. From his point of view we see De Franco who knows what Tyler is going to do. Tyler shoots him and blood flies everywhere. Tyler exits the restaurant and enters a car driven by Lipton. As Tyler tries to come down after his fake assassination Lipton pulls a gun and tells Tyler that the reason for the plastic on the seat is that he didn't want to get blood on the upholstery. They fight over the gun and the car crashes into an abandoned building. A homeless man tells them that they can't park there.

Tyler finds a phone and calls Mason telling him that Lipton tried to kill him. Mason tells Tyler to stay put. Another man wants to use the phone and Tyler goes to a niche to stay out of the rain. Cops drive up and shoot the man in the phone booth and then tell Mason that "the package was delivered, but to the wrong address." Tyler then knows that Mason is part of the plot to kill him.

Keith comes home and Tyler hustles her into the hallway, checking to see whether she's been followed. He tells her that Lipton and Mason are trying to kill him. She tells him that they want him as a patsy for the killing of De Franco. Two thugs pull up in a car outside Keith's apartment.

The next morning Tyler and Keith wake up to another morning in which the problem of Mason trying to kill him hasn't gone away. As Keith opens the drapes she is shot.

Tyler ducks and waits for the assailant. They have a grand battle and Tyler finally prevails killing the assailant with an iron.

He lifts Keith's body off the floor and places her on the bed.

The scene shifts to the bedroom of an NYPD detective Lt. Leo McCarthy (Brian Dennehy) who is having a tough time waking up.

McCarthy makes it over to the scene of what appears to be a double homicide and his assistant Mickey (Joe Grifasi) fills him in on what they know.

Back at police headquarters McCarthy finds that the dead assailant was both an ex-army guy as well as ex-NYPD.

Meanwhile, Tyler reads the paper to see that the police are searching for De Franco's killer. He calls his assistant Andy (Martha Gehman) and tells her to bring his makeup kit to the boathouse on Central Park's model sailboat lake.

He sees from a window that she's been followed. He tells her to take a sailboat and hand it to the man. When the man tries to put it into the water, Tyler shoves him in and he and Andy run off. The man gets out of the water and chases them. They find an abandoned tunnel with a trapdoor that leads to a series of underground tunnels. The man has to abandon the chase.

McCarthy and Mickey go to Tyler's apartment and find that the bullet holes in the doorway monster duplicate the bullet holes in De Franco's corpse. McCarthy think that the assassination might have been staged.

The next morning Tyler and Andy emerge from the underground tunnel looking like the other homeless who also climb up the stairs to emerge onto a busy New York street.

While Tyler and Andy are losing themselves in the crowd, McCarthy and Mickey go to see Mason. He doesn't convince McCarthy that he knows nothing about the killing of Keith's assailant, who happens to be one of the men who works for him at WPR.

Mason tells Lipton to meet with Tyler. Getting into his car, Tyler loops a wire around Lipton's neck and tells him to drive to an abandoned stretch of road. Taking Lipton's gun, Tyler opens the trunk and Andy gets out replaced by Lipton. After a series of trunk bashings Lipton finally agrees to divulge Mason's address.

Later, Tyler and Andy find the F/X truck in the impound yard and after a series of explosions are able to drive it away. However, they are followed by Mickey who has been sent to surveil the truck in the yard.

McCarthy following a hunch calls Mason at home and finds out the De Franco is still alive.

A series of traditional car chase scenes (sidewalk driving, beef carcass encounters, pedestrians freaked) the F/X truck escapes with Mickey stopping to give aid to an F/X dummy that Andy dropped out of the back of the truck. In an abrupt stop Tyler snookers Andy and drives off without her.

At police HQ McCarthy is suspended for his supposed indifference and concentration on the WPR aspect.

Tyler drives the F/X truck to Mason's house. Mason, De Franco and the rest of the gang are inside playing cards and watching TV.

Tyler rigs an electrical charge to the entry gate and zaps the guard, temporarily dimming the interior lights. The men inside wonder what's going on.

Another guard investigates the entry gate. Tyler zaps him with a balloon. De Franco wants to leave but Mason tells him to sit down.

Outside, Tyler is setting more traps.

McCarthy drives up to the entry gate and sees the two men that Tyler has rendered hors de combat. He drives off with red light flashing on top of his car.

Tyler makes entry with his bag of tricks. He cuts the wires to the alarm system as well as the house lights. De Franco yells that Tyler is inside the house.

Tyler breaks a vase and lures two of the thugs upstairs. By placing a screen that shows his image he suckers one of the bad guys to shoot the other. Then he places a trip wire for the second. And does him in with a blunt instrument.

Mason yells for one of the men, but there is no answer. De Franco opens his gun case and takes out an Uzi machine gun.

McCarthy flags down a NY State Police cruiser. As De Franco panics and fires at the French doors, McCarthy and the state trooper have to duck to avoid the bullets.

Tyler staggers in through the doors with what appears to be fatal wounds.

A helicopter approaches the house. The State trooper tells McCarthy that they don't have helicopters.

De Franco runs into an electrically charged screen that disrupts his pacemaker, a device that Tyler knew about from De Franco's original prosthesis-making. Mason extracts a key from De Franco who expires.

Tyler confronts Mason who tells him that the key is worth ten million—all the money the feds stole from the mob. Tyler has another switch to pull on Mason. He leaves the Uzi unattended. Mason picks it up. Tyler tells him that in one hand are the bullets for the gun and in the other is Crazy Glue with a thousand and one uses. Shoving Mason out the door he adds another use.]

The police outside see Mason with the gun. He pleads that it's not what they think. Too bad. They kill Mason.

McCarthy sees Tyler who appears to be dead again. "Too bad, Rollie I liked your movies."

In the morgue, one of the body bags has movement.

Too see the surprise ending requires another six or so minutes of film and is definitely worth waiting for. Not only does it resolve the problem of the key but it also sets up the premise for F/X 2. Enjoy the film, but then that will be a given.

Gallipoli

Watching a grizzled old-timer clock a young man running in the dirt of the Outback in Australia hardly seems to be what the fratricidal war in Europe in 1914 is all about. Yet, the rivalry that a racer engages in epitomizes the rah-rah attitude of the men who fought that First World War.

Archy Hamilton (Mark Lee) is the runner being timed. He turns in what Jack (Bill Kerr), the old timer thinks is a winning time for the upcoming race.

One of the horsemen who works on the spread is antagonistic to Hamilton telling him that boxing is a man's sport not running. Hamilton bets the cowhand that he can make it back to the ranch house faster on foot than the man can on a horse. As Hamilton starts to put his boots on, he's told that he has to run barefoot. To even things up he tells the cowpoke that he has to ride bareback.

Hamilton beats the cowhand, but in the process tears skin off his feet making the old timer fearful that he has thrown away a chance at winning the big race.

At the race venue, it is part carnival, part sentimental with the singing of "Tipperary" and all competition.

One of the racers who signs up for the money race is Frank Dunne (Mel Gibson). He is told by the officials that there's a man in the race who has beaten Dunne's time in a previous race. Dunne hands over the entry fee nonetheless.

The race is on and Hamilton wins. After the race an army contingent appears willing to sign up men to fight for king and country.

Hamilton attempts to join the light horse unit but the same cowboy he beat exposes the fact that he's only 18. The recruiter turns him down.

Later, in a tea shop, Dunne shows up and apologizes to Hamilton for being so curt after the race. He is hungry and finishes the food that Hamilton doesn't want. Dunne suggests that they go to Perth where Hamilton can try again to enlist.

To get to Perth, they hop a freight train. Hamilton asks whether they are going to Perth. Dunne says where else can it go?

In the morning they find that they have been marooned in the middle of the outback. A lone railroad employee tells them that the next train will be by in two week's time.

Hamilton says that's not good enough and he starts across the barren desert. Dunne follows until they are almost done in. Hamilton sees dung and runs to catch up with a wanderer with a camel. The man hasn't heard of the war, but says that they are only 10 miles from a station.

Hamilton and Dunne whoop and holler about beating the desert and go to the station where they clean up and meet the family. Hamilton is joyous about joining the light horse, but Dunne is still unsure of getting involved with the army.

At Dunne's father's place the father protests his son's fighting for England when his grandfather was executed by the English. Dunne says he won't fight for the English; rather he'll just keep his head down.

William Behr Mueller

Hamilton gets a fake mustache and beard from Dunne and Hamilton shows Dunne a few of the rudiments of riding so they can join the light horse together.

At the recruiting ground, Hamilton performs admirably, but Dunne cannot get his horse to move and is denied admission to the light horse contingent.

In a pub the soldiers are rousted by an NCO. Hamilton leaves with the other soldiers and Dunne has to wish them goodbye.

The men of the light horse parade through Perth before they board a ship that will take them to the war.

All the Australian soldiers arrive in the Australian training camp in Cairo, Egypt. Football keeps them busy until they are set free to explore the shops. Before so doing, however, they have to endure a medical explanation of what kinds of diseases they might expect to find as they seek some "horizontal refreshment."

One fiasco leads to another until they find some very loose women who are ready, willing and able to give them what they want at a reasonable price.

After their sojourn in the shops and bordellos, they march into the desert.

At rest the infantry receives a rousing pep talk about how they are going to go up against the light horse.

During the exercise Hamilton and Dunne meet again.

Later at a dance given by the Australian nurses they enjoy an evening of great fun, champagne and womanly companionship.

Hamilton takes a note to his commander, which reads that they will embark for Gallipoli in the morning.

Arriving at night, the men of the light horse and infantry make it to shore without significant casualties.

Integrating into the already large Anzac (Australian/New Zealand) force Hamilton and Dunne move into the trenches.

The British are about to land a large supporting force and that landing requires the Anzac forces to mount an attack on the Turkish positions to divert Turkish fire and give the British troops the ability to land safely.

The Australian commander tells his subordinate commanders that they must succeed in their diversion to give the British troops the necessary window to land.

In the trenches Hamilton convinces his commander to use Dunne as his runner because Hamilton has waited so long to be a part of the fight.

The communication line goes dead and Dunne must brave machine gun fire to get back to the command headquarters where the commander emphasizes the need for the attack to proceed even though the Turks have the high ground and are slaughtering the men as they go over the top of the trenches.

Dunne gives that message to the commander who thinks about it and asks Dunne to get confirmation from the general in charge.

Dunne again braves the Turkish bullets and gets a reprieve from the general.

William Behr Mueller

He runs back to the commander, but is not in time and the attack proceeds with the same result.

Hamilton is the last casualty in the attack.

This film portrays accurately the collegiate spirit the men exhibited before they experience the horrors of trench warfare. It also shows the inflexibility of the high command to understand exactly what kind of certain death they were sending their men into. The command chain was not only inflexible on the ground but the overall commander remained on board one of the ships in the channel rather than coming ashore. That alone was enough to compound the slaughter on the ground.

This film should have a disclaimer about the brutality and horror that will be seen toward the end of the film so be forewarned that the battle scenes are realistic and bloody.

Hard Times

A freight train comes into the frame. Chaney (Charles Bronson) looks out of the door of one of the boxcars at a car stopped at a crossing. As the train slows Chaney hops off with his valise and jacket. He starts walking into town.

At an eatery he finishes his second cup of coffee and sees some men get out of cars and walk into a warehouse. He leaves the eatery and goes into the warehouse stopping short of the action to observe the spectators who want to see blood.

There two fighters wait to fight while the bets on the outcome are taken by both promoters. Speed (James Coburn) wants his man to win and shouts encouragement as the fight progresses. His man, however, is not up to the task and is beaten.

The next day Speed enjoys oysters on the half shell. When he gets up for another half dozen Chaney sits at his table. Speed looks Chaney over as Chaney takes one of the oysters. He tells Speed that he has six dollars and wants Speed to bet it on the outcome of the fight he will have. Speed takes a chance on Chaney, and they return to the same venue.

The man who was victorious in the previous fight taunts Chaney. Chaney makes no rejoinder. When both men step into the fight, Chaney knocks the other man out with one blow. Speed is amazed that he finally has a real winner.

Speed wants Chaney to accompany him to New Orleans where he says they can make a lot of money. When the train arrives in New Orleans, Speed's "fiancée," Gayleen Schoonover (Maggie Blye) meets him and Chaney. Speed thinks Chaney will accompany them, but Chaney says he wants to see the city. He tells Speed that he might see him around.

Chaney gets a rundown room for a dollar and a half a week.

Chaney finds Lucy Simpson (Jill Ireland) in a hash house and takes his coffee over to her booth. After a few words he convinces her to let him walk her home. She tells him that her husband is in jail and that she has no prospects. He turns away and says he might see her around.

The next morning Speed sits on the balcony of a two-room rental in the French Quarter and hears the doorbell buzz. It's Chaney. Speed tells his woman to get out of bed, they have company.

Chaney is there to make a business deal with Speed. He tells Speed what the percentage will be on all the receipts. Speed tells him that it isn't done that way. Chaney starts to walk away and Speed relents.

Speed picks up Poe (Strother Martin) who has been his fight handler in the past. He introduces him to Chaney and they all become partners.

Speed and Chaney show up at a barge where another fight is being staged. The promoter is a cut above Speed and Jim Henry (Robert Tessier) defeats his opponent, giving Chaney a chance to see Henry's fighting technique.

Speed needs money to be able to get a fight that has big money involved. He goes to Le Beau (Felice Orlandi), a loan shark, and gets a thousand minus the 50 for interest and there will be 50 for each day the loan is outstanding.

With his new money Speed goes to Gandil (Michael McGuire) and tries to buy in but Gandil ups the ante to three thousand. The only way for Speed to get the additional two grand is for him to take Chaney out to one of the Cajun cook-outs to have another pickup fight.

After negotiating the odds, Chaney has no trouble with Pettibon's (Edward Walsh) fighter. But Pettibon isn't going to give up the money because he says Chaney is a ringer. Speed tries to get Pettibon to cough up when one of Pettibon's boys pulls a gun.

Chaney, Speed and Gayleen leave but Chaney has a plan to get the money.

They drive around until it's dark and then stop at a roadhouse. Pettibon and his boys are enjoying the evening when Chaney comes in, takes the gun away from the owner, knocks out any others who want to throw him out and then demands the money from Pettibon. Pettibon refuses and says that Chaney won't use the gun. To show Pettibon that he will he pistol whips Pettibon who then gives up the money. Chaney asks whether Pettibon owns the place and when the answer is yes, Chaney empties the pistol at various parts of the roadhouse before leaving.

Speed visits the promoter with the money and gets the odds and the deal for Chaney to fight his man.

The warehouse that the fight will take place in has a cage for the fighters. There are balconies with men waiting to see the bloody fisticuffs and making plenty of noise in the meantime.

William Behr Mueller

Speed, Poe, and Chaney show up and the money is given to a third man to hold.

Chaney approaches Henry who has a smile on his face indicating that he thinks the fight won't last long and will be resolved in his favor.

Henry is wrong as the fight progresses and Chaney bests him. Speed gets the wad of cash and it appears as though he will not only be able to repay the loan but will have some spending money to boot.

All the partners and their lady friends adjourn to a saloon, but Speed has the gambler's itch and he finds a crap game in a seedy warehouse. He shoots all his money but as with many gamblers doesn't know when to stop and he loses all the money he won in the fight.

The scene shifts to a ferry boat and Speed tells Chaney that the man who Chaney will fight doesn't have the long arms that have been reported. He also tells Chaney that since he beat Jim Henry so badly, fights will be harder to get and the odds won't be nearly as good.

Gandil is in the oyster business and Speed and Chaney visit him at his oyster processing plant. Gandil offers Speed five thousand dollars for a half interest in Chaney. Chaney tells Gandil that he has to talk to him not Speed. Gandil complies telling Chaney that he used to have the best street fighter in the city but now he doesn't and that is not what he wants. Chaney turns him down and they leave.

Speed turns up at a whorehouse and satisfies his needs.

When he arrives back at his rental, the leg breakers from Le Beau, the man he owes money to, are there with sledgehammer and proceed to bash Speed's car before telling him that Le Beau wants his money.

We go to the ferry landing. Chaney and Poe wait for Speed. He tries to convince Chaney to accept Gandil's offer. Speed pleads with Chaney and then tries to shame him into giving him more of the money they won in the fight. Chaney leaves.

Next we see Gandil and Henry wait for a train to pull in to the station. Street (Nick Dimitri) gets off the train and hands his bag to Henry who at first refuses to carry it.

At Gayleen's place she asks Chaney whether he ever gets scared when he does his work. He replies that he doesn't think about it. She tells him that she wants more than a casual relationship. He tells her "Suit yourself" and leaves.

In a pool hall, Chaney enjoys a beer. Gandil, Street and Henry come in and Gandil tries to convince Chaney to take the five thousand. Street menaces Chaney, but Chaney walks by him saying he won't do it for free.

When Speed arrives back at his rental, he is abducted by Le Beau's men. At Le Beau's place Gandil tells Speed that he will pay off his debt if he can get Chaney to take the deal.

Poe tries to get Chaney to take Gandil's deal to save Speed, but he won't do it.

Meanwhile Speed waits for Chaney to show. Henry hopes that he won't so that he gets a chance to take revenge on Speed for all the remarks he's made since the fight.

William Behr Mueller

Chaney goes back to Gayleen's place and she tells him not to drop by anymore. He leaves her without another word.

Poe shows up at the Oyster plant and they wait to see whether Chaney will show up for the inevitable fight.

For his own reasons, Chaney does show up. Poe announces the arrival by throwing a hammer through the office window. Speed is released and shakes Chaney's hand. Speed tells Gandil that no matter what he does he's always going to smell like fish.

Chaney gives all his money to Speed who gives it to Gandil. The fight begins. Each man throws punches, kicks and finally Gandil wants Street to use steel bars to finish Chaney. Street refuses and loses the fight.

Chaney demands his money. Speed, Chaney and Poe leave the oyster plant.

On a railroad siding, Chaney gives Poe money to take care of his cat and then gives Speed money to take care of Poe. He strides off without saying anything.

Speed and Poe decide to go to Miami, with Chaney's cat.

If you are averse to street fighting then you'll probably have a tough time watching this film. On the other hand if you enjoy excellent performances, especially by James Coburn you'll want to spend the hour and a half with these characters.

King Kong

An interesting departure from today's films is the "Overture" that takes the first four minutes before the Radio Pictures logo appears. As it was recorded in monaural it really doesn't add much to the film (even if Max Steiner composed it).

The side of a ship sets the scene to begin the film. As the man asking about Carl Denham boards the ship there is an energetic discussion among Denham (Robert Armstrong), First mate John Driscoll (Bruce Cabot) and Captain Englehorn (Frank Reicher). Denham says that he wants to make a picture like no other that has been made before. To do so he needs an actress.

Roaming the streets of New York, Denham looks over the women applying for assistance at the Women's Home, but doesn't see what he needs. He then goes to a fruit vendor and as he's talking to the man a woman, Ann Darrow (Fay Wray), grabs an apple and the grocer says he's going to call the police. Denham buys him off and takes Darrow to a restaurant where he buys her food and coffee and tells her that he has a job for her as well as a sea voyage. She demurs and then accepts.

Aboard the ship *Venture*, Denham tells Reicher that they are seeking an island that is on a crudely drawn map in his possession. The ship sails toward the South Seas. Driscoll dismisses Darrow as a nuisance.

Meanwhile Denham makes a test film of Wray in which she has to be absolutely terrified of something. She succeeds and satisfies Denham.

Driscoll appears to be less dismissive of Darrow and then becomes infatuated with her.

William Behr Mueller

The ship drops anchor in view of the island with a centuries old wall and a skull mountain. The crew takes a movie camera and side arms and goes ashore.

There they see a strange ritual taking place. Denham tries to get film of it but the chief sees him and the ritual stops as he and some other members of the tribe approach Denham, Driscoll and Darrow. The rest of the crew stay alert to any hostility on the part of the natives.

The chief tries to buy Darrow. Denham refuses and tells all of them to head back to the boat and return to the ship.

Later that night Darrow sits by the bulwark.

Unknown to her or any of the rest of the crew, the tribal chief and his minions approach the ship and kidnap Darrow.

They take her to the ritual place where she is to be offered to Kong.

The men on the ship search it for Darrow but not seeing her and noticing that there are fires near the great wall they take rifles and go ashore.

All the tribesmen and women tie Darrow to the two pillars of the sacrificial altar and then retreat to the top of the wall.

Denham, Driscoll and the others see what is happening to Darrow. A giant ape has taken her off the altar and moves back into the jungle.

Denham and the others open the gate and follow the ape.

The ape's footprint staggers them at its size. They continue to follow the ape and Darrow.

A stegosaurus feeds in the distance. They attempt to avoid it, but it sees them and charges. They use one of Denham's gas bombs to disable the beast and then shoot it to finally put it down.

The next problem they encounter is a lake, so they build a raft to try to cross it. A water creature (actually a brontosaurus) sees them, overturns the raft and proceeds to kill many of the group. The rest flee for their lives.

Kong puts Darrow in a tree perch and has a battle with an allosaurus. Kong defeats the beast but not before the tree with Darrow is downed. After dealing with the allosaurus, Kong frees Darrow and continues his journey to Skull Mountain.

The group follows Kong and Darrow, but Kong sees them and sends most of them to their death at the bottom of a ravine. The only survivor is Driscoll. Denham has also hidden from Kong and Driscoll tells Denham that he will continue to follow Kong and will signal Denham about Kong's whereabouts.

Denham returns to the wall and the rest of the crew.

Driscoll follows Kong and Darrow into Skull Mountain. Darrow is on a ledge and is attacked by a large creature. Kong fights the beast while Driscoll and Darrow observe the battle.

After dealing with the creature, Kong takes Darrow up to a higher ledge where he starts removing some of her clothes (the nearest to a racy scene that the censors would allow in 1933). Driscoll steals behind Kong as Kong is fighting a Pterodactyl that has attempted to carry Darrow off. Driscoll takes Darrow and climbs down a liana, but Kong is not to be so easily relieved of his blond prize. He starts pulling up the vine.

William Behr Mueller

Just as Driscoll and Darrow are about to be captured by Kong they drop off the liana and fall into the lake below.

Out of the water, Driscoll and Darrow run for their lives and make it back to the wall.

Kong pursues his prize and pushes and pounds on the barred gate until the bar cracks and Kong is released.

Everyone flees to the beach and Kong follows, killing many of the tribal people in his rampage.

On the beach Denham throws a gas bomb at Kong and Kong is completely disabled. Denham tells the crew that they have disabled the 8th Wonder of the World. He will share in the profits from exhibiting the beast.

In New York City, crowds enter the theater where Kong is to be shown. Denham wants to show the patrons that without Darrow and Driscoll the beast they are about to see as proof of their adventure would not have been captured.

The audience is properly awed by Kong's size. Denham asks the reporters to come on stage to document the beast. They use flashbulbs that torment Kong. When he thinks that the flashbulbs mean danger to Darrow he breaks the chrome steel chains that hold him secure. Panic ensues and Kong batters down part of the theater wall to escape.

After rampaging in the city including smashing an elevated train and dropping a woman from high up in a hotel, Kong finds Darrow and disables Driscoll. He takes Darrow and seeks a better refuge.

Driscoll and Denham go to the police and Driscoll finds out that there is nothing that can be done with Kong climbing the Empire State building. Driscoll says they can use airplanes.

Kong makes it to the top of the Empire State building and after he deposits Darrow on another ledge, the airplanes arrive. Taking shots at Kong they continue to rake him with machine gun bullets. He is taken by the blood coming from his neck and chest. Still in a destructive/protective mood, Kong grabs one of the airplanes and sends it crashing to the ground.

More attacks and finally Kong is so weakened he loses his grip on the building and falls to the street below.

Driscoll climbs up the ladder to reunite with Darrow.

On the street, Denham views Kong's body. He says "The airplanes didn't kill him, Beauty did."

For a black and white film made in 1933 this story still holds up. The rear screen projection for the very small beasts was done well enough that it still appears seamless. The beasts reflect the dramatic needs of the picture (even if there are factual errors in their behavior). The acting is commensurate with the story and Fay Wray has a lot of screaming, which can get a little over the top, but Armstrong's portrayal of a movie mogul who will do anything to get something that the public has never seen before appears to be a good representation of what drives directors and producers to plan and execute a "project."

Memphis Belle

Cumulus clouds in a blue sky. Fly through them. Pan down to some soldiers playing a rough version of American football. Watch as they check out the B-17's returning from a bombing run over Germany.

Cut to the base commander, Col. Craig Harriman (David Strathairn) trying to count the returning airplanes while he's being cajoled by public affairs Lt. Colonel Bruce Derringer (John Lithgow) about the 24 missions that the Memphis Belle has completed.

The ground crews are worried about the last airplane to return to base. Finally they see it, but one of the landing gear has not deployed and there appears to be problems with one of the engines.

The pilot makes a relatively good landing and the airplane skids on the grass finally coming to a stop. Then in an instant the airplane explodes and the entire crew is incinerated. Shock appears on the faces of the ground crew and the other airplane crews that have witnessed the landing and explosion.

Harriman attempts to get his aircrews off going to bomb Bremen again, but higher command will not budge.

After an uproarious evening dancing in a hangar with some of the flight crews attempting and in one case succeeding to have sex with one of the English women at the dance.

The next day the aircrews are briefed on the mission.

After the briefing we follow the crew of the Memphis Belle to their bomber. They all climb aboard and in the cockpit Capt. Dennis Dearborn (Matthew Modine) starts the checklist for starting the engines. His co-pilot 1st Lt. Luke Sinclair (Tate Donovan) follows the instructions given by the taciturn Dearborn and its apparent that there is no love lost between the two men.

The signalman sends up a flare telling the crews that they can get ready to taxi out.

Then a jeep rolls up to the planes telling them that the target has been obscured by cloud cover. The Belle's navigator Lt. Phil Lowenthal (D. B. Sweeney)is convinced that he will be killed on this run and suffers from a ferocious hangover. He climbs out and attempts to sleep on the bomber's wing.

One of the crew members who has farm experience shows a local farmer who is trying to coax a machine into action just off the parking apron how to run the machine.

Finally, the target clears and the crews climb back into their bombers. The pilots start their engines.

Soon they are aloft and flying on their trajectory toward Bremen.

Flying into clouds, things appear to be going smoothly, but as the clouds break up Dearborn and Sinclair see another bomber just above them so Dearborn puts Belle into a dive to escape what could have been a midair collision.

The guns are tested and as the plane reaches ten thousand feet the crew goes on oxygen.

William Behr Mueller

German fighter planes attack the bombers. Some are dispatched by the "little friends" (P-51 fighters) and then the fighters depart to conserve fuel leaving the bombers to proceed into Germany without fighter escort.

Flak begins almost immediately and when the bombardier Lt. Val Kozlowski (Billy Zane) cannot see the target, Dearborn decides that they have to turn around to see whether the target will clear. Lowenthal attempts to push the switch that will jettison the bombs, but he is wrestled away by Kozlowski.

Belle resumes the bombing run, but Kozlowski still cannot see the target. Tension is high as nobody wants to push their luck with the flak and the fighters by making a third run over the target.

Finally the clouds clear, Kozlowski can focus on the target and releases the bomb load with all the other planes in the squadron following suit.

One of Sinclair's unfulfilled desires is to shoot at a German fighter. He makes an excuse to be able to go to the tail gunner position. The tail gunner continues to work on his model of a B-17 as Sinclair takes over his gun position.

A German fighter attacks Belle from behind and Sinclair is able to disable the fighter. Unfortunately the fighter dives into another B-17 cutting it in half. Sinclair is horrified that his victory has cost the lives of the men aboard the halved airplane.

More fighters attack Belle and parts of the plane are shot away, one of the waist gunners is severely wounded and an engine on the right wing catches fire threatening to burn though the wing and destroy the Belle.

Dearborn tells Sinclair now back in the co-pilot position that they have to dive the plane to try to put out the fire.

In the dive the plane exceeds the maximum allowable speed before the fire is extinguished and the two pilots put all their strength into pulling out of the dive.

Back at the base in England, all eyes are turned to the sky to count the returning airplanes. One by one they arrive, but the Belle is nowhere in sight. As the seconds tick by the men's faces become even grimmer.

On the Belle Kozlowski attempts to use his skimpy medical knowledge on the wounded gunner, but he thinks that it's a hopeless effort and tries to persuade the captain that they have to strap a parachute onto him with ripcord in hand and push him out through the bomb bay. The men don't agree with Kozlowski and finally persuade him to continue with his efforts at trying to stabilize the gunner.

The plane is barely controllable and they are losing fuel from a punctured wing tank. Over the English Channel, Dearborn tells the crew they have to lighten the plane and that they can throw their guns overboard since they won't need them.

The final problem is that one of the wheels will not deploy. Will it be a replay of the first one-wheel landing that ended with a fireball? Crew members use the mechanical crank to try to lower the resistant wheel.

The plane limps toward the base with rudder partially shot away, ball turret destroyed and the men in crash positions. Co-pilot and navigator continue to crank on the stubborn wheel.

William Behr Mueller

Just before the plane touches town on the runway the wheel fully deploys. The landing is safe and the men have completed their last mission, as has the Belle.

This film has all the realism that you could expect in a first-rate Hollywood production. The instrument panel, interior, guns, and turrets all work and add to the feeling that you are in a B-17 on a war mission. For airplane enthusiasts, military buffs and anybody wanting an in-depth look at men at war, it's hard to think of a film that will provide more or a better look at the men who tried their best to defeat Hitler and the Nazi war machine.

Mud

Two boys on a quasi-Huckleberry Finn adventure hardly make for exciting or at least interesting movie-making and viewing, but there is more to this film than first meets the eye and in comparison to other shoot-em-ups and blow-em-ups it's a refreshing take on getting performances on film.

Ellis (Tye Sheridan) waits for his friend Neckbone (Jacob Lofland) to bring his flat-bottomed outboard to the houseboat on which he lives. As he sneaks out of a window he passes by another window through which he sees his mother and father discussing something. He hopes he hadn't been spotted. Neckbone shows up and they speed away from the bayou on which they live.

The object of their journey is a heavily forested island. Beaching the boat they walk into the woods and find a boat that had been strangely lifted into the trees. They scale the tree and enter the boat. It will be their special place.

Looking through some of the items that have been strewn about, Ellis finds a sack with fresh bread. The boys know that someone has been living in the boat. They leave and go back to the boat.

Ellis sees tracks in the sand and they investigate, but find the tracks disappear. They turn to see a man by their boat and they go over to him.

Mud (Matthew McConaughey) greets the boys and they warily begin a conversation with him. They want to know what he's doing on the island and whether he's been living in the boat. Ellis is more concerned with establishing ownership of the boat, but Mud tells them that possession is nine-tenths of the law. Ellis will have none of it.

In the boat, the boys continue to ask Mud about the why of his being on the island, and he is still not ready to reveal who he really is or why he's there. He does tell them that he needs help from Tom Blankenship (Sam Shepard) who lives across the river from Ellis and his family.

The boys take Blankenship to the island but he will not help Mud since he thinks that he has lost his way.

The boys take Blankenship back to his house and then Ellis has to undergo a chewing out from his father, Senior (Ray McKinnon) for being late. They sell fish from an old pickup with an ice chest. Ellis asks his father what he was talking about with his mother Mary Lee (Sarah Paulson). He doesn't get a straight answer.

Ellis sees one of the girls in his school getting roughed up and he goes to her rescue and knocks down the boy who was tussling with her. They set up a date.

He is a reluctant 14-year old when it comes to asking her to be his girlfriend but she relents after giving him a kiss. It thrills him to no end.

Ellis and his mother drive along a road and stop at a roadblock. One of the officers shows them a wanted poster with Mud's picture on it. Ellis has to lie when asked whether he's seen the man, but then asks what he's done. The officer tells them to drive on without saying anything about Mud's picture on the wanted poster.

Back on the island, Ellis and Neckbone tell Mud that they've seen his picture on a wanted poster. He has to tell them the story of how he killed a man because of how his girlfriend, Juniper (Reese Witherspoon) was being treated.

Mud tells them that he needs the boat to get away and because the boys are somewhat larcenous at heart they agree to help him get the boat out of the tree and make it seaworthy.

Stealing what they consider worthless junk from various boatyards around the town they haul a lot of material to the island for Mud to use to rig a means of lowering the boat out of the tree.

What he needs is a chain saw and the boys bring him one.

Mud rigs a swinging perch and saws off one of the limbs that supports the boat. He is overjoyed that the limb came down without striking him.

One of the problems that Ellis' mother and father have is that their houseboat doesn't belong to his father and it is going to be repossessed by the family member who is the rightful owner. His father takes the occasion to tell Ellis to watch out for women because they will only lead you on to rack and ruin.

Ellis finds his father's advice to be on the money as the girl May Pearl (Bonnie Sturdivant) ignores him during another situation in which Ellis attempts to stop what he thinks is an invasion of his special relationship with May.

Back at the island, Mud tells the boys that he needs a motor for his boat.

William Behr Mueller

They sneak into a boatyard and haul away a large outboard motor and take it to the island.

Back at Ellis' place Senior comes unglued when he tells Ellis that some men spotted Ellis and Neckbone stealing the motor.

Ellis pleads the case that he thought the motor was worthless.

Senior proceeds to lambaste Ellis for depriving a man of his means of making a living just as he was being deprived of his means of making a living when the houseboat is repossessed.

Mary Lee steps in and tells Ellis that he is to apologize to the motor's owner, return the motor and never do anything like that again.

He tells his father that he can't return the motor.

Back on the island Mud gives Ellis a note to give to Juniper who Ellis spotted in a market when he was getting food for Mud.

Ellis and Neckbone drag their ice chest with fish along the balcony of a motel. A black man tells them that he wants no fish. Finally Ellis knocks on Juniper's door, opens it and finds that she is being roughly treated by a man who knocks Ellis down. Neckbone comes to the rescue holding up sacks of fish, telling the man that they are only trying to sell the fish.

The man leaves and Ellis gives Juniper the note. She reads it and then tells the boys she will buy some fish.

As the story progresses, King (Joe Don Baker) and his cohorts kneel to pray that the man they are seeking will meet his death for killing King's son.

The boat is finally ready to be launched, but Ellis berates Mud for leaving Juniper and for deceiving the boys.

Ellis runs away, followed by Neckbone. Ellis falls into the pit with the poisonous snakes. Neckbone runs back to get Mud.

Mud takes Ellis into his arms, asks Neckbone for the time and writes it on Ellis leg with the snakebite. They race back to Neckbone's dirt bike.

Mud takes the bike and drives to a hospital, telling the emergency crew that the boy has snakebite. When one of the attendants tries to get information from Mud he leaves.

Mud goes to the motel where Juniper is staying and waves good-bye to her.

After Ellis recovers, Mud sneaks into his room, but that is when King and his friends decide to have their vengeance.

A shoot-out of monumental proportions ensues with Blankenship sharpshooting from across the river.

As Mud runs out and tries to escape by jumping in the river, a final shotgun blast appears to do him in as he doesn't surface.

Ellis is devastated that Mud has been killed.

After all the police work has been done, Blankenship takes the boat away from the island. He goes below and sees Mud wrapped in a large bandage.

Back in town, Ellis gets a nod from May Pearl and that makes his day.

William Behr Mueller

Be prepared for a slow beginning with a lot of character development and for some this will not be their cup of tea, but for others it will be two hours of good entertainment.

O Brother, Where Art Thou?

To the sound of some clanking, a graphic tells us that we are about to witness the story of a wanderer, harried for years on end...

The camera slowly pans to show us the clanking sound resulted from a chain gang breaking rocks, and singing a dirge to remind themselves where they are.

The film title appears and the camera moves to a long shot of the chain gang with a solo voice singing "The Big Rock Candy Mountain." Suddenly three of the chain gang who are escaping pop up in the field. The front credits appear.

The three men shackled to each other attempt to steal a chicken at a nearby farm. They are successful and cook the bird, but there are pursuers after them signified by the baying of blood hounds.

Another graphic tells us that the story was inspired by Homer's *The Odyssey*.

The three jump a passing train and Everett McGill (George Clooney) makes it aboard and asks the hobos if any of them is a "Smitty." Delmar O'Donnell (Tim Blake Nelson) climbs aboard as Everett asks more questions. Pete Hogwallop (John Turturo) can't make it and he drags the other two off the train. Everett is somewhat discouraged and Delmar apologizes for not being able to be counted on. Everett maps out a plan, but Pete didn't elect him to be the boss of the outfit. Everett counters that the leader should be the one with a capacity for abstract thought.

William Behr Mueller

With no decision as to the leadership, a handcar appears and they climb aboard. The driver (Lee Weaver) is blind. He says he works for no man and has no name. Everett quips that those reasons might be the impediment to his finding gainful employment. The old man tells them that they will find a fortune but not the one they seek. The three men have a long and difficult road in front of them with strange sights such as a cow on the roof of a cotton house. They listen but don't know what to make of his ramblings.

After leaving the handcar, Delmar asks how the old man knew of the treasure. Everett tells him that the blind have certain properties that compensate for their lack of sight. Pete pipes up that the blind man said they wouldn't get their treasure because of the "ob-stack-cles."

In front of them a boy with a rifle shoots at them and asks if they're from the bank. Delmar replies that they are not from the bank. They walk up to Pete's cousin, Wash Hogwallop (Frank Collison), whom he hasn't seen for 13 years. Wash comments that they probably want those chains knocked off.

At dinner, Wash spells out what happened to Mrs. Hogwallop. The ruse is to keep the boy from knowing that she "r-u-n-n-e-d-o-f-t."

Delmar comments on how good the stew is. Wash says that he slaughtered the horse last Tuesday and he's afraid she's startin' to turn.

After dinner they listen to "You are my Sunshine" on the radio. Everett spends time combing his hair using Dapper Dan hair pomade. The commercial pleads the merits of Pappy O'Daniel's

(Charles Durning) flour. Everett asks whether Wash has a hair net. Mrs. Hogwallop left some in the bureau.

Later that night, the authorities show up and Everett says "Dammit, we're in a tight spot." He accuses Wash of turning them in. Pete will have none of that, but Wash admits so doing because he has to look out for himself and family because "they've got this Depression on." Pete tells his cousin that he will kill him, but machine gun bullets interrupt his tirade.

The trio sees a flammable fluid splashed against the barn. The liquid is set alight. A torch lands in the barn. Pete throws it back and it sets fire to the police van with all the ammunition and explosives.

A car runs through the flames and into the barn. The Hogwallop boy tells them to get in because he's gonna "r-u-n-n-o-f-t." Telling Pete that he isn't the boss of me, he drives the car through the flaming barn wall.

Kicking the boy back to his father, Everett goes to a general store to get a part for the disabled car. He also needs to buy pomade. The clerk shows him Fop, but Everett says he's a Dapper Dan man commenting on how the store appears to be two weeks from every other point on Earth.

In the woods, Pete laments that they only have four days to get to the treasure before it goes to the bottom of a lake. Delmar offers roasted gopher to Everett.

Everett's plan is to trade the watch he lifted from Wash's bureau for a car and enough gas to get to where the treasure is. Pete doesn't take the theft of his cousin's watch lightly.

William Behr Mueller

Delmar comments on the white robed people walking through the woods. "'Pears to be some kind of congregation."

"Come on brothers, let's go down, down to the river and pray." The song appeals to the curiosity of the trio and they follow the congregation.

As Everett makes a snide comment about the mental capacity of the congregation, Delmar wades toward the preacher and the full immersion baptisms he's performing. He tells the others that all his sins and transgressions have been washed away. Pete follows suit.

The sheriff with the sunglasses has found a tin of Dapper Dan pomade as well as the hairnet and gives both to a bloodhound.

Driving off, Everett tells Pete that his sins may have been washed away but that was only for the preacher not for the law. Further discussion reveals that Pete doesn't like the smell of Dapper Dan.

"Baptism," Everett remarks. "You two are dumber than a bag of hammers."

Delmar tells him to pull over to give the colored boy a lift. His name is Tommy Johnson (Chris Thomas King) and he carries a guitar case.

Delmar asks Tommy what he's doing in such a god-forsaken place. Tommy says that he had to be at that crossroads at midnight to sell his soul to the Devil.

Everett says that he's the only unaffiliated one among them. Delmar is appalled that Tommy traded his soul. Tommy says he wasn't using it.

Pete asks Tommy what the Devil looks like. Everett provides the classic view, but Tommy says that he's as white as them with hollow eyes and a deep voice.

Tommy reveals that he's going to Tishomingo to sing into a can because there's a man there who pays well for that activity.

At WEZY the quartet goes for an audition with a semi-blind man who runs the station. The blind man asks who they are. Everett tells him that he's Jordan River and his friends are the Soggy Bottom Boys with songs of salvation to soothe the soul.

The men sing into "the can" and their song becomes a hit. Their payday is $10 a piece.

Outside, Delmar attempts to get Pappy O'Daniel interested in singing, but Pappy tells him that he's not there to sing. Pappy's staff tries to get him to press the flesh, but Pappy says they're "mass communicatin'."

Sitting around a campfire listening to Tommy play a lament, the trio dreams about the huge amount of money that's waiting for them to find it. Pete will become a restaurateur, Delmar will redeem the family farm, but Everett didn't have a plan when he stole the money.

The sheriff and his men show up and holler at the barn where they think the trio is hiding. The trio watches from the woods. The barn is fired and the men run off.

As they walk on a country road, Pete says that no one is going to pick them up. Everett addresses Pete's hopeless negativism asking him to consider the lilies of the goddamn field.

William Behr Mueller

They turn to see a dust cloud behind them. It's a car driven by George Nelson (Michael Badalucco) and he is pursued by the police. They get in the car. Nelson asks whether they're bad men, but Delmar tells him that he and Pete were saved.

As the police get closer, Nelson steps on the running board with a Thompson submachine gun and flaunts the law with huge bravado.

Skidding into town Nelson tells them that they're going for the record: three banks in two hours. He tells the customers in the bank that "Jesus saves, but George Nelson withdraws."

One of the patrons says that he's "Baby face" Nelson. That remarks infuriates Nelson and Delmar has to calm him down.

Around another campfire Nelson appears to be depressed. Everett explains that a thrill-seeking personality will be on top of the world one minute and then in the depths in another. Nelson leaves.

A farmer in a field outside of WEZY watches a sound truck with a tiny man come by with the message that Homer Stokes will sweep the state clean as the small man sweeps the bed of the truck.

Inside the studio a man asks where he can find the Soggy Bottom Boys. He tells the blind cracker who manages the studio that they have to sign the Boys before the competition does.

Walking through the woods, the trio appears to be on the way to Satartia. They steal a pie from a farm windowsill but Delmar leaves a cash payment as they run off. They consume the pie in a bar. Everett throws the newspaper he was using as a plate into the fire. A headline states how famous the Soggy Bottom Boys have become and asks the question "Who are they?"

Hitchhiking, the trio has to duck because a prisoner truck trundles by.

 A customer requests a record of the Soggy Bottom Boys, but the clerk tells her that they just can't keep a supply in stock. As their fame grows they still have to live on the rough side, ducking rain and using camp fires.

They finally get a ride to a store that carries Dapper Dan hair pomade. They leave the store and steal a man's car who has just entered the store.

Pete tells Delmar to stop playing the guitar. He jumps out of the car and sees women singing and doing their wash. The men are transfixed by the singing and the obvious physical charms of the women. Each chooses one and the day progresses into night as the singing progresses and white lightning lubricates the encounter.

Morning and only two of the men are around. Delmar sees Everett's feet and Pete's neatly laid out clothes and shoes.

Everett shouts for Pete to stop his shenanigans while Delmar observes something under Pete's shirt: it's a toad that hops out into full view. Delmar screams and tells Everett that the sirens loved him up and turned him into a horney toad. Delmar chases the Pete/toad and catches him. He talks to the toad trying to make it understand that it's Delmar who's holding him.

In an upscale restaurant Delmar tells Everett that it's not right to keep Pete in a shoe box. Delmar refuses to accept Everett's explanation of Pete's comeuppance.

William Behr Mueller

Showing how much ready cash the duo has interests Big Dan Teague (John Goodman) sitting alone at another table. With an eye patch he strains his uncovered eye to take in the scene with Everett and Delmar.

Big Dan convinces the boys to box up their lunch and hie off to more suitable environs.

In another part of the restaurant, Pappy O'Daniel worries about Homer Stokes and the upcoming election. His son suggests they get some "reform" but Pappy reminds him that they are the incumbent.

Under a tree Big Dan chews on a chicken leg. After he tells them that he proposes to give them a lesson in psychology he breaks off a large-limb from the tree they're sitting under. Big Dan proceeds to use the limb on the boys, but Delmar won't stay down and he fights with Big Dan. Big Dan downs Delmar and then proceeds to squash the Pete/toad and after he's finished with that nasty bit of work he steals their car and drives off.

Iris out.

Pete is strung up and being horsewhipped until he reveals where Everett and Delmar are heading. The pursuer with sunglasses (at night) tells Pete that they're experiencing "sweet summer rain. Like God's own mercy." The pursuer halts the hanging.

In the back of a stake truck, Everett and Delmar ride a back road discussing the treasure and whether it's right to dig it up without Pete. As they pass another chain gang, Pete is one of the prisoners.

The scene changes to a political rally for Homer Stokes (Wayne Duvall). Everett and Delmar get off the truck in front of the rally. Everett recognizes the girl singers as his daughters. He tells them what their name is but they tell him that it's been Wharby ever since he got hit by that train. He discounts their story and they add that their mother has a new beau. Everett tells them that he's the only daddy they have; he's the pater familias. They tell him that he's not bona fide.

Everett goes to the five and dime and confronts his ex-wife Penny (Holly Hunter). They argue about the result of his being sent to the penal farm. He tells Penny that he's back and he wants to reunite with her and his six daughters. Vernon T. Waldrip (Ray McKinnon) doesn't want to be pushed out of the picture. A fight ensues in which Everett is thrown out of the "Woolworth."

Watching a movie, Everett tells Delmar not to trust a woman and if he follows suit the time he's spent with Everett will not have been ill spent. "Woman is most fiendishly devised creature to bedevil the days of man," opines Everett.

The lights dim and a chain gang is brought in to watch the picture show. Pete is part of the gang and tells Everett and Delmar not to seek the treasure because it's ambushed. Delmar tells Pete that he thought he was a toad.

The scene changes to a mansion with Pappy O'Daniel discussing how much of a friend to the farmer he is.

In a prisoner barracks, Pete laments and then Everett readies a bolt cutter to free Pete. Outside Pete tells them how he was treated by the Pursuer and his men. Then he confesses to having spilled his guts about the treasure. Everett tells them

William Behr Mueller

that there "ain't no treasure." That revelation infuriates Pete who only had two weeks left on his sentence. At the end of the tussle they hear the chanting and the light from a KKK ritual in which Tommy will be the sacrificial victim.

A grand wizard dressed in a red costume starts a chant and the legion of followers starts a ritualized march. Pete sees the noose on the gibbet and says they have to save Tommy. The trio knocks three of the K's out of the picture, taking their robes, confederate flag and shields as the grand wizard continues his spiel saying that the ladies expect those gathered to protect them from darkies, Jews, Papists and any other smart ass who says they descended from monkeys.

Big Dan Teague lifts his hood to inspect the men who are leading Tommy to the noose. The trio tells Tommy that they are going to rescue him. He says nobody can rescue him because the Devil has come to collect his due. Big Dan strips the trio of their hoods and they have to use the flags to keep the K's at bay. Homer Stokes lifts his grand wizard hood and asks who made them color guards?

Using the bolt cutter to snap the wire holding the flaming cross that falls on Big Dan the quarter uses the diversion to make their escape.

At another political rally, Pappy O'Daniel muses about hiring Vernon T. Waldrip away from Homer Stokes to run his campaign. His toadies agree that if you can't fight 'em, join 'em.

Watching from a distance, our heroes come to another leadership crisis when Delmar appears to favor someone else as leader rather than Everett.

Homer Stokes and his little man drive up, throw their K costumes in the back seat as Stokes says "What I wouldn't give to get a hold of those agitators."

Inside, our heroes dressed in long beards prepare to add music to the festivities. Delmar leads off "In the Jailhouse now" as Everett attempts to get Penny to notice him. He tells her that his plan is to be a dentist because he knows a guy who will print him a license. Pappy tries to get Waldrip to change allegiances while Pete yodels.

Delmar introduces "A man of constant sorrow" and Everett is amazed at the crowd's reception.

Stokes reveals his affiliation with the K's and the crowd reacts negatively to him, so much so that they pelt him with food, finally driving him out of the hall.

Pappy climbs onto the stage and dances as the Soggy Bottom Boys continue singing. He also pardons the trio and tells them that they will be his brain trust in his second administration. He says that they will now sing "You are my Sunshine."

Outside, Everett reunites with Penny. Waldrip is shut out. Everett suggests they marry with the ring that Waldrip bought, but Penny will have none of that. There won't be a weddin'. Everett throws his hat on the ground as a parade leading George Nelson walks down the street. He looks forward to being electrocuted.

Walking down a road the boys listen to Everett reminisce as the Pursuer captures them and prepares to hang them. Everett tries to tell the Pursuer that they've been pardoned. It's been on the radio. "We ain't got no radio," says the Pursuer.

William Behr Mueller

The men make their peace with the Almighty. Saved by a mighty wall of water, they swim around cans of Dapper Dan and other detritus. Finally they surface and cling to a coffin, much like Ishmael at the end of Moby Dick. Everett chides them for believing a miracle saved them.

Everett sees the cow on the roof of a cotton barn.

We see Everett and Penny walking together. He says that all's well that ends well. He shows the ring he got from the roll top desk, but Penny disavows it. He tries to explain how difficult it will be to go back since the lake is very deep and very large. She doesn't care; it's not her ring. The children follow their parents singing. One of the daughters stares at a blind man pumping a handcar on the railroad tracks.

The Coen brothers take potshots at a variety of institutions in the film: criminal justice, the law, business, politics, marriage and the family. It's all in good fun, providing a chance for sparkling dialog and interesting character development. The plot may be a bit too coincidental, but the ragged edges don't show because the action is too fast. You will find the time and money spent on this film to be well worth it.

On the Waterfront

Be prepared for a gritty black and white film when you start watching this one. The "message" delivered in this film deals with conscience and humanity.

As the film opens some very beefy men leave a waterfront shack designated as the headquarters for the local longshoremen's union. They don't appear to be dock workers in the usual sense. Terry Malloy (Marlon Brando) and Johnny Friendly (Lee J. Cobb) the union boss are among them.

Malloy finds out what the men have in mind when he shouts up to Joey that he's found one of the kid's pigeons. Joey goes up to his coop on the roof and subsequently Malloy sees him fall off. Thugs make light of the killing as Malloy says he only thought they were going to "lean" on Joey. Charley Malloy (Rod Steiger) tells his brother to forget about Joey. Pop Doyle (John Hamilton) and a policeman arrive and the cop wants some information, but the dock workers are fearful and refuse to give him any information. Edie Doyle (Eva Marie Saint, in her introductory role) wants to know who killed her brother. Father Barry (Karl Malden) provides some comfort but she wants more.

In what appears to be a mob-style gathering with piles of money spread out on a table, Friendly and Charley Malloy talk about one of their biggest worries: the investigation being conducted by the Crime Commission. Friendly tells his "ironboss" who doles out the assignments for men working on the ships to give Terry Malloy a slot in the loft where he doesn't have to do anything except, perhaps, count the number of items that are being offloaded. Charley pacifies Friendly about his brother's misgivings about Joey's murder.

William Behr Mueller

Terry Malloy goes up to Joey's coop to find out that some of the neighbor kids have been feeding Joey's pigeons.

On the dock two men from the Crime Commission show up to talk to Terry, but he won't have anything to do with them. Then the clout of the ironboss shows when he doles out the counter tags that allow men to be employed on the ship. The mood of the crowd is ugly because they know that only privileged men will be given the tags. Finally, even with police protection, the crowd moves to intimidate the ironboss and he throws all the rest of the tags into the crowd that scramble to get one of the very valuable items.

Edie and Father Barry show up at the docks to try to find out who murdered her brother Joey. She witnesses the riotous behavior of the men scrambling for the tags as the priest tries to keep her safe. She is concerned for her father who has worked on the docks for years to be able to keep her in a school run by nuns. He is roughed up in the melee. Barry keeps her from being trampled by the mob of men.

Inside the ship Charley confronts Terry and tells him that he has to keep his mouth shut about anything that the men from the Crime Commission might ask him.

Later Barry holds a meeting with the few longshoremen who show up at his church. Terry Malloy attends as a spy for the mob. Thugs from the mob roust the men and drive them out of the church.

Terry and Edie become acquainted as they escape from the mob scene at the church.

Back at Edie and Pop's apartment, he wants her to return to the school so that she will not become further involved with either Joey's murder or Terry Malloy.

Edie goes up on the roof to see Terry. She sees that he is caught up with his pigeons, which is a different side from what she's seen so far. He takes her for a beer and they find out more about each other. A rowdy wedding interrupts their tete-a-tete.

Friendly confronts Terry about the church meeting and tells him that he failed to report on what really happened there and how it's related to the Crime Commission. Charley tells Terry to wise up.

The next day in the hold of another ship, one of the outspoken longshoremen is killed by "accident" and Father Barry gives a most impassioned speech about why the men should stand up for their rights. Terry listened and appears to be convinced.

Later, Terry goes to Father Barry and tells him that he wants to help. Barry tells him that the only way is for him to confess to Edie about his role in her brother's death.

Trying to convince Edie when ship's whistles interrupts his speech means the only words that Edie hears are abhorrent to her because of Terry's involvement in her brother's death. She leaves.

On the roof, one of the Crime Commission investigators confronts Terry again and he refuses again to "rat" on his brother or the other members of the mob.

Friendly tells Charley that Terry has to be shut up or killed.

William Behr Mueller

In one of the classic movie scenes, Charley tries to talk to Terry about his loyalty to the mob. The subject of the thrown fight Terry regrets comes up. "I coulda been a contender. I coulda been somebody" is the heartfelt pronouncement that Terry gives his brother. Charley's response is to give Terry a gun because he will need it. Terry leaves the cab and Charley goes on to see Friendly and the boys.

Terry goes to see Edie and even though she doesn't want to see him he breaks the door to her apartment and brutally takes her for a kiss. She responds.

Outside, they find Charley's body. He's been shot a number of times.

In a bar Terry confronts members of the mob, but Father Barry interrupts the scene and demands the gun from Terry. He has to wrestle with Terry to get the gun.

Sometime later, the Crime Commission hearing takes place and Terry points the finger at Friendly who tells him that he won't work on the docks again and he will be lucky to stay alive.

After the hearing, Terry goes back to his pigeon coop to find that all the pigeons have been killed, something that both saddens and infuriates him. Edie tries to keep him from seeking revenge but he says he isn't going to hurt anybody he just wants his "rights."

Terry shows up at the dock when the ironboss tells the collected men that everybody works. As they stream into the warehouse, only Terry is left and the ironboss tells him to show up again tomorrow for the same treatment.

In the union shack, Friendly confiscates all the guns from his hoodlum gang because they are an honest union.

Terry knows that the only way he will get his "rights" is to confront Friendly, which he does with all the men who were going to work on the ship as his audience.

Friendly becomes infuriated at Terry's taunts and they fight. Terry is getting the best of Friendly when Friendly's thugs comes to his rescue and savagely beat Terry.

Father Barry looks at how badly beaten Terry is but tells him that if he can walk to the warehouse they may have "lost the battle, but have a chance to win the war."

Terry staggers into the warehouse with all the men following to end the film.

With the bad guy turning good and solving one of the worst problems on the waterfront, you get a sense that maybe with determination and courage some of the most egregious wrongs in the world can be righted. Gritty, emotions in a raw state, and lots of tough looking actors make this film captivating. Hard hitting speeches by all the principal actors add to the drama and make it a worthwhile viewing experience. Check it out.

Remo Williams

A New York cop (Fred Ward) enjoys his lunch hour. He sees a man running past, but since the man doesn't appear to be involved in a crime he continues with his lunch. Then two other men are in hot pursuit of the first man. That changes the dynamics of the situation and the cop moves his patrol car into the warehouse where the three are located. He turns the lights on and sees that the two have cornered the first man and are assaulting him.

After more fights and car chases, Ward is chased down by an unknown assailant, and he is taken away by ambulance.

What has happened to Ward has been a "recruitment" to find out whether one of the military contractors really is going to provide the ultimate weapon. Harold Smith (Wilford Brimley) is the recruiter and he wants to find out whether Grove Industries is on the up and up with respect to the military contracts they are working on.

But first, Ward has to be schooled in advanced Korean martial arts. To do that he is introduced to Chiun (Joel Gray) who is a man that can dodge bullets (a nifty trick).

Chiun puts Ward, who has been renamed by Conn MacCleary (J.A. Preston) because of a stamped impression on the bottom of a pot: Remo Williams, through a grueling series of tests to bring him up to the physical strength that will be required for what will become a high thrills adventure.

We meet Major Rayner Fleming (Kate Mulgrew) early on and she appears to be an officer who will take no guff from anybody.

On the weapon proving ground, one of Grove Industries' weapons malfunctions and kills the soldier who was firing it. This "accident" reinforces Fleming's suspicions about Grove Industries.

Meanwhile, Remo and MacCleary break into Grove's heavily fortified plant to find the ultimate weapon. Remo finds it and it destroys the room in which it sits.

He and MacCleary have to escape before they are caught by the security guards. Unfortunately, MacCleary is shot and killed, but Remo escapes.

Fleming pursues her investigation regarding Grove as Remo, dressed in camo fatigues, enters the proving ground. He is immediately attracted to Fleming.

In a series of near misses, Remo and Fleming escape the fatal end that Grove and the commanding officer have in mind for them.

In a final aerial log ride, Remo escapes the machine gun fire that Grove attempts.

Remo lands on a beach and Chiun has a speedboat ready for their escape. Fleming makes it to the boat, but Remo is cornered by Grove who thinks he will have his revenge for all the trouble that Remo has caused.

The ending of this film is in keeping with the other aspects that cause a suspension of disbelief. If you want to have a couple of hours of good entertainment with the good guys coming out on top then check out this film.

William Behr Mueller

Safe

Be prepared for Luke Wright (Jason Statham) to clean house a number of times in this film.

The two stories that intertwine are those of Wright and Mei (Catherine Chang), a brilliant phenom whose memory is photographic and ultimately very valuable to almost all the players.

Wright is an ex-cop who turned to cage fighting to lose the ignominy of being kicked off the NYPD. He's not aware of the precise reason for his termination, but suspects it was due to the corruption of top of the line officials as well as the detectives who were also on the take. Not taking a dive in his latest fight has cost one of the Russian gangs a huge amount of money and they want retribution.

At the same time that Wright is getting out of the very sticky situation with the Russians that includes having his wife murdered, Mei's memory is essential to Han Jiao (James Hong) the boss of the Asian gang who wants the number that Mei has memorized. He also wants her memory as it will be invaluable to shake down the various businesses in New York's Chinatown. She can list the supposed cash flow versus the actual cash flow as she is walked past some of the shops in Chinatown. When one of the shopkeepers is confronted with the skim he's been taking he is shot by Mei's "guardian," Quan Chan (Reggie Lee). He explains that killing the shopkeeper is part of business. She is appalled at such brutality.

Meanwhile a group of Russian thugs would like to steal Mei away because they know that she has memorized the combination of a safe that contains thirty million dollars. Captain Wolf (Robert John Burk) would also like to have the cops' share of the protection money be paid on time; to assure that end he has to obtain a passport for Mei.

As Mei is sheparded around Chinatown, Wright goes from one flop to another finally trying to help out another down-and-outer whose feet have become infected from not having shoes. Wright gives him his shoes. But the shoes don't have the necessary effect and Wright finds the man dead in the cot next to his the next morning.

Wright wants to get away from the possibility of befriending someone else as he goes down the street to stop in a convenience store. Another down-and-outer bumps into him as he is ready to enter the store. At the register he fumbles for money to pay for his goods, but his wallet is gone. He laughs at what he thought was only an unfortunate bump into another of New York City's homeless. The manager asks a police lieutenant in the store to eject Wright.

Outside the detective recognizes Wright. Wright is set upon by his ex-colleagues and beaten severely. They tell him that he is an outcast and that if anyone befriends him or vice versa they will snuff that person.

The Russian boss has Mei and wants her to divulge the number that she's memorized. He also wants to know who she's told about the number. The woman who has befriended Mei tells the boss that she's told no one. Unfortunately she is not believed and is killed, shocking Mei once again at the brutality of the people she has to deal with.

William Behr Mueller

What appear to be uncorrupted cops demand entry into the Russian sanctorum, but they are denied. Outside the NYPD sends hundreds of cops to the hotel where the Russians are holed up.

In the chaos, Mei finds a way to leave the room the Russians have her in and finally leaves the hotel. The Russian boss sends his men out to find Mei.

Meanwhile Captain Wolf is tracking Mei using all of NYPD's resources. He finds that she is at the hotel where the Russians are.

Wright is at the end of his rope as he stands next to the edge of the platform that overlooks the subway tracks. As he is about to end it all he notices a Chinese girl, which turns out to be Mei trying to escape from all the Russian gang members who are searching for her. She boards a subway car and Wright follows the Russians who are after Mei.

On the subway car Wright uses his cage fighting techniques on the Russians, but loses Mei in the aftermath. He follows her but she is lost in the crowd of subway passengers who leave the platform.

Downfallen that he has lost Mei we cut to a scene in which the detectives who are on the take find Mei and abduct her under the pretense of helping her.

Wright rescues Mei but the Russian mob enters the scene and Wright has to take the detective's car on a wild chase to try to escape the Russians.

None of those who are trying to capture Mei understand that it is Wright who is their nemesis.

Wright takes some of the money he took from the detectives he beat up and robbed to get out of his homeless duds and then he and Mai take a hotel room in one of New York's finest. He prevails upon Mei to reveal the number, which is the combination to the safe with the multi-millions. All is not well, however, because they have been tracked. When Wright finds out that they have been tracked he looks for and finds the tracking device in Mei's cell phone. They have to get out of the hotel before he is killed and Mei is recaptured.

The Asian gang invades the hotel and turns it into chaos.

Wright has to escape some NYPD officers and that gives the Asians the chance to retake Mei.

Wright commandeers a car and then abandons it and takes a taxi. The driver asks the destination and Wright looks in one of the Russian's wallet and gives the driver the address, which happens to be the hotel where the Russians are. He also uses the Russian's cell phone to call the Russian boss to make a deal.

Meanwhile Wolf is reamed by his boss, Mayor Tremello (Chris Sarandon).

The rest of the film shows Wright's cunning and how he gets revenge on the men who caused him to lose his job with the NYPD.

Fortunately the murder and mayhem in this film is not quite the edge of the seat stuff that revolts many viewers and it is also not thrown in for good measure. Statham is the kind of actor who appears to enjoy being cast in roles that require him to experience pain as well as dish it out.

William Behr Mueller

Seven Years in Tibet

A man dedicated to mountain climbing finds peace but is harassed and imprisoned along the way.

That one sentence explanation will do for a capsulated and truncated description of this film.

A harrowing sequence captures the viewer as Heinrich Harrer (Brad Pitt) saves Peter Aufschnaiter (David Thewlis) from certain death after the latter slips and goes over a cliff. Harrer has to put all his effort into holding onto the rope so that his climbing partner will not die.

The summit of the mountain is Harrer's goal but it is not to be as Aufschnaiter orders the expedition to go back down the mountain. The order does not sit well with Harrer and he trails the others as they move back to a lower level. One of the guides gives Harrer a picture of the Dalai Lama telling him that it will protect him.

At the base camp, the climbers are arrested since England has gone to war with Germany and they are enemy aliens in Northern India.

Spending time in the British prisoner of war camp, Harrer has only one thing on his mind as that is to escape so he can continue his climbing. Time after time he escapes only to be returned to the camp.

Finally Aufschnaiter and some of the others plan to escape and their method is poo-poohed by Harrer. Aufschnaiter wears a British officer's uniform and the others are shoe-polished brown to appear as lowly road workers.

When they have left the confines of the camp, they discard the camouflage of the cart and take out packs and food for their journey to China.

Harrer goes off on his own.

In a series of brash temple thieving Harrer gets enough food for his journey.

As Harrer is vomiting some food that was not agreeable, Aufschnaiter arrives and they decide to try to make the Chinese border together.

Needing food, Harrer tells Aufschnaiter to barter his watch for food. The watch was a present from his father and he doesn't want to lose it; nonetheless they need food and he trades the watch.

Later, Aufschnaiter finds that Harrer had three watches and confronts his partner expecting an apology. Harrer tells him that they were only throw aways and meant nothing. Aufschnaiter stomps off telling Harrer that the reason he always travels alone is that no one can stand him for very long.

As the story of the mountaineers unfolds a child who is the Dalai Lama goes through various rituals connected with his exalted status in the Tibetan society.

After many arduous miles of walking Harrer and Aufschnaiter arrive in Tibet where they are turned away but finally are given access to a local chieftain. In the process of planning an escape, Harrer convinces their guides to wear iron ice boots. In the ensuing chase the guides lose footing because of the iron boots and Harrer and Aufschnaiter escape once again.

William Behr Mueller

Trudging over the very rough terrain Aufschnaiter's feet become incapacitating. Harrer massages them and they continue their journey, making camp under a shelter half. Armed bandits raid their camp and take them prisoner. Harrer has a knife that he plants in the leg of a guard and both men steal horses and ride away with bullets flying after them.

The escape is not complete as both horses die, the last one providing a bit of food for the two men.

In dire need of food they see farmers sowing seed, but there is nothing for them.

Shortly, a group of pilgrims comes their way and the two men join the group that is on its way to Chando to pray in the presence of the Dalai Lama.

Passing the guards at the entrance to the town, the men spot an old woman who sets out food for her dogs. They greedily eat the dog's food and the old woman attempts to chase them away, but an advocate steps in and takes them back to his quarters.

As they wait they are cleaned up and shaven while the advocate attempts to get legitimacy for them from the Dalai.

Enter a female with a catalog of men's clothes. She is a seamstress and measures the men for the clothes she will make.

Outside, Harrer shows her how to rappel and she says that walking up a mountain is a fool's pleasure. When Harrer shows her news clippings of his exploits, she explains the differences in their cultures.

As the men stroll around town they meet the man who provided the western clothes they now wear. He bids them adieu with *auf wiedersehn* saying they will meet again.

The man who has benefitted the two Austrians is a secretary to government ministers and is questioned by the Chinese mission chief as to why he is displeased with the Chinese gifts to Tibetan monasteries. The mission chief attempts to recruit the secretary but is rebuffed.

Outside Chinese soldiers unload weapons.

Harrer rips one of the pockets of his jacket and goes to the seamstress's house. He finds Aufschnaiter there and it appears as though both men are interested in the seamstress.

At a vendor who says that ice skates are for cutting meat, they explain the true use for the skates and then on an ice pond show her how to skate. During the episode she falls and Aufschnaiter helps her up much to the disgust of Harrer, who it appears has lost the love duel.

As the ice skating proceeds, the Dalai uses his telescope to achieve a kind of pleasure by proxy.

Later, Harrer writes a letter to his son and the same sentiments that he writes could be applied to the Dalai.

In an audience with the Dalai, Harrer is asked whether he can build a movie house for the Dalai. He will have to visit the Dalai every day so the boy can find out things about the world that Harrer comes from.

William Behr Mueller

As the digging progresses the workmen find worms in the ground and tell Harrer that they wish to stop hurting the worms.

The Dalai tells Harrer to think of a solution to the worm problem. He does and the workmen sift through the dirt and remove the worms. As they save the worms, Harrer teaches geography to the Dalai and then gives him a driving lesson.

Various play activities fill the screen including kite flying.

That night a comet fills the sky accompanied by pots and pans being banged while old women shout "Evil omen."

The old women were right as Mao Tse Tung becomes Chairman and vows to return Tibet to the Chinese Mother Country.

The Tibetan government will have none of Mao's yearnings and they expel all the Chinese from Tibet.

As Harrer works on the movie house, the Dalai learns his Tibetan lessons.

Showing Christmas to the Tibetans, Harrer distributes gifts as an ad hoc band plays Christmas music. Later the crowd dances to modern dance music.

Aufschnaiter opens his present and it turns out to be the watch that he pawned those many miles ago for food. A note from Harrer thanks him for his friendship.

Without warning the Chinese invade Tibet. Three generals bring a message of reconciliation to the Dalai: autonomy and religious freedom.

The Chinese have no intention of fulfilling the general's words as they send two armies to attack the Tibetan frontier. The secretary is now the governor of Chando and vows there will be no surrender as long as he is governor.

A Chinese night attack with rockets and mortars throws the Tibetans into a confused mass. After the massacre the governor requests permission from Llasa to surrender. With the surrender the Chinese occupation begins.

Harrer confronts the governor and returns the jacket gift, a great insult to a Tibetan. He wishes the governor a long life so that he may endure the shame of betraying his culture.

In a touching confrontation, the Dalai tells Harrer that he should return home to be a father to the son he has never seen.

Then it's time for the Dalai's enthronement.

Harrer leaves Tibet and in 1951 takes the music box given to him by the Dalai and presents it to his son.

Later, Harrer teaches his son to climb and the film ends with them on a mountain with the Tibetan flag firmly planted by their sides.

You will marvel at the scenery in this film as well as the topnotch performances of all the major actors. Seeing how a culture was destroyed by a ruthless dictator will leave you appalled but not bereft of hope that it may someday be reconstituted.

William Behr Mueller

Shooter

Gunnery Sergeant Bob Lee Swagger (Mark Wahlberg) and his observer wait to ambush an Al Qaeda-like machinegun mounted four-wheeler. They are somewhere in the Middle East. A command post with military types controls their activity and Swagger thinks they will send a helicopter for extraction when the mission is completed.

As Swagger is given the OK to open fire he does and kills the machine gunner. A convoy of evidently good guys passes the disabled four-wheeler. The observer calls in the completed mission, but then he sees a large convoy of hostiles hot on the trail of the good guy convoy. To slow the hostiles down Swagger takes out some of the gunners in the hostile convoy. That opens a pitched battle between Swagger, the observer and the hostiles who use small mortars to target Swagger and his observer.

The observer tries to call the command post but the officer in charge has already wrapped up the operation because they were deep inside territory that was not only hostile but had not invited them to begin with.

That means that Swagger and his observer will have to make their way out of the predicament they're in.

To add another problem a heavily armed helicopter starts shooting up their position. Swagger tries to use his sniper rifle on the chopper but can't seem to hit it. On another chopper run his observer is killed. Now the helo has to be taken out if Swagger is going to have any chance of escaping.

He fires again and again and finally hits the rotor housing and the chopper goes down.

The screen dissolves to a graphic that reads "Thirty-six months later." Swagger is in the woods with a large dog that appears to be his only companion.

The dog growls at an oncoming SUV as the two of them share a beer.

Col. Isaac Johnson (Danny Glover) and two other men start to walk toward Swagger's house. He confronts them and Johnson asks to have five minutes of Swagger's time.

Johnson prevails upon Swagger to join in the hunt for an assassin that will target the president at one of his speaking engagements. Swagger finally agrees because of his core belief that America and especially its president must be protected.

To sharpen his own sniper skills, Swagger shoots a can of Dinty Moore stew from a distance of 600 yards, blasting it to smithereens.

Next Swagger flies to the east coast and checks out various locales including the main one in Philadelphia.

He provides detailed data on what the assassin will do to be able to make his shot. Using binoculars, Swagger checks the wind as he and Johnson and some other men wait for the president to arrive at the event.

A uniformed policeman comes into the group and Swagger has to remind him that his gun holster is not snapped shut.

William Behr Mueller

As Swagger sees the president go up on the stage he tells Johnson that he must take the assassin down now.

At the moment the policeman opens fire on Swagger wounding him and knocking him out of the window onto fall breaking structures below. The policeman continues to fire at Swagger with Johnson telling the others in the room to kill Swagger.

Staggering from his wound, Swagger makes it over to FBI agent Nick Memphis (Michael Peña) who has been given a position to monitor; one which the agent thinks is all too quiet.

Shortly Swagger confronts the agent, disarms him and finally handcuffs Memphis to part of the overhead bridge.

Swagger takes Memphis' car and is chased by the men sent by Johnson. Local police join the chase.

Moving to the back seat of the car in a car wash, Swagger attempts to staunch the blood from his wounds. He reaches into the trunk after cutting through the seat to get the first aid kit.

Johnson and the rest of the police and FBI search for Swagger. He appears to be cornered and then he drives the car off a wharf. As the police search for him he snags a ride on a barge downriver.

Coming ashore on some riprap Swagger staggers toward a pickup truck in storage and is able to start it and resume his escape.

While the FBI agent who Swagger disarmed is interrogated by his superior, Swagger blows the lights at a convenience store and gets supplies he needs to add IV fluid to make up for his blood loss.

Memphis tells his superiors of how battlefield wounds were treated and that is exactly what Swagger is doing.

Memphis becomes suspicious of the reasons why the FBI is hunting Swagger and watches the video of the assassination attempt.

Meanwhile Swagger goes to his observer's widow Sarah Fenn (Kate Mara) and asks her for assistance since he has nowhere else to go. She agrees to get the supplies he needs.

Memphis analyzes the shooting and finds out that nothing adds up. Then he finds out that the cop who shot Swagger was himself killed.

Fenn expertly ministers to Swagger. He has strange dreams while Memphis continues to investigate the facts of the shooting. When he is sufficiently recuperated Fenn gives him a .22 caliber rifle.

In a church steeple, Memphis finds holes in the floor that gives him an idea about the weapon used in the shooting.

Swagger recuperates as Memphis finds out exactly what weapon was used in the shooting: an electrically controlled high power rifle.

Fenn meets with Memphis wearing a blond wig. Swagger watches Memphis leave and then two local cops attempt to subdue Swagger, but he disarms them and gets away again.

William Behr Mueller

Memphis runs the VIN given to him by Fenn and he finds out that high level clearance is needed to be able to access details on the VIN.

Memphis is kidnapped and tortured and is about to be killed with his own gun, when Swagger shows up and dispatches the nasty guys who were about to kill Memphis. Swagger uses the .22 caliber rifle and soda pop silencer.

Johnson sends his men to get Fenn.

Swagger and Memphis visit an old rifleman who is willing to help them and in the process reveals something that brings up a memory in Swagger about a man who is more ruthless than God: Michael Sandor (Rade Serbedzija).

Johnson proposes Sandor as bait to trap Swagger. He approaches Senator Meachum (Ned Beatty) for permission to bring 24 assassins into the country.

Two of Johnson's thugs capture Fenn although she is able to shoot one of them.

Swagger and Memphis prepare an arsenal to deal with what Swagger knows will be a full assault on him.

One of the assassins plays with Fenn while Memphis and Swagger prepare their assault on the building where Sandor is waiting as bait.

Swagger enters the building. Sandor waxes philosophical about power. He is obviously playing for time. Surprisingly Sandor commits suicide and then a general melee happens with the body count reaching epidemic levels. In a déjà vu situation Swagger destroys a helicopter and he and Memphis escape.

From Bozeman, Montana Swagger thru Memphis brokers a deal to exchange the info from Sandor for Fenn. It's another setup but Johnson has some surprises in store.

Another band of nasty brothers sets off in pursuit of Swagger at his meeting with Johnson on the snowy mountaintop. In a snow suit he does in Johnson's hit men.

Fenn kills her captor. Meachum demands Swagger's side of the bargain. He offers Swagger a job and then philosophizes about the good his destruction of a village brought to the region in Africa.

The FBI arrives in choppers. Swagger destroys the tape he made of Sandor's confession.

Swagger is taken back to Washington to face charges that he was the sniper who killed the archbishop.

He shows how the firing pin was not in the weapon and the bullet that was a match had been fired at a can of Dinty Moore stew.

Johnson tells Swagger that he wins—again. Swagger is unshackled and is told that he is free to go.

Sometime later at Meachum's lavish country home with a cozy fire burning, he and Johnson revel in how well they pulled off the coup and no one is the wiser because the incriminating tape was destroyed. Meachum says "The truth is what I say it is."

Swagger cleans house. When no one is above room temperature, Swagger smashes the gas line and exits the house. Shortly the entire place erupts in a ball of flame.

William Behr Mueller

Swagger moves over the hill and Fenn picks him up in her car to end the film.

If you want to see revenge exacted for duplicitous behavior this is your cup of tea. You will also be introduced to what is meant by "a conspiracy" at the highest level. Wahlberg's abilities border on the superhuman, but in the end he's just a guy who wants to do things the right way—even if it means he has to eliminate some of the nasties who would have done him in if they were competent enough.

The Day the Earth Stood Still

Simulated 3-D letters provide the credits for this foray into 1950's science fiction. Accompanied by Bernard Herrmann's eerie soundtrack, you couldn't ask for a better beginning to an early alien vs. Earth film.

A radar operator sees a blip that makes him jump to attention and ask for a senior officer. Other military establishments around the globe also react to the extremely fast movement of the unidentified flying object.

Numerous commentators provide radio coverage of the unexplained phenomenon stoking fears that whatever it is it does not have peaceful intentions.

In Washington, D.C., many pedestrians look to the sky to see the pulsing disk-shaped object appear overhead. It appears to be heading toward the Capitol Mall.

The crowds on the mall flee the giant disk as it settles onto the ball fields.

Police and army units race to the landing site, setting up a perimeter with tanks, artillery and cocked and ready side arms and rifles.

Nothing appears to happen until a ramp slides out from the disk and part of the dome opens.

A "spaceman" emerges from the dome saying that he has come in peace. He walks toward the armed and ready soldiers.

As he walks he reaches into his metallic suit to take out a cone shaped object.

One of the men on the tanks reacts to what he thinks is a weapon and shoots the alien. Soldiers crowd the alien and an enormous robot emerges from the disk and uses a deadly beam from his open visor to melt all the tanks, artillery pieces and rifles of the soldiers before the space man tells him to stop the destruction.

An officer rolls up in a Jeep and calls for an ambulance to take the space man to Walter Reed Hospital.

At the hospital the space man is visited by an aide to the president. He finds out that the space man's name is Klaatu (Michael Rennie). Klaatu tells the aide that he must speak with all the representatives of the nation states on Earth. The aide tells Klaatu that such cooperation is probably not in the cards, but he will try anyway.

Klaatu is locked into his room to await the return of the aide who reads him the responses from various heads of state who will not attend any meeting unless the meeting is held in a place of their choosing.

Klaatu says that before he makes a decision as to Earth's fate he should get out and get a better understanding of the people he will pass judgment on. The aide says that the military does not want Klaatu to leave the hospital.

When a guard and nurse enter Klaatu's room they find him gone.

Klaatu has appropriated the clothes and bag of a Major Carpenter. He sees a "room for rent" sign and enters the building. As Bobby Benson (Billy Gray) sees Klaatu, he reacts and the others in the room who have been watching the TV coverage of the disk turn to ask him what he wants. He tells them that he saw the sign for the room.

Shortly, he meets Bobby's mother, Helen (Patricia Neal) and then is shown to his room next to Helen's.

At breakfast the next day, Klaatu finds that his neighbors in the rooming house have very strong opinions as to the danger the disk and the space man pose. Helen, however, takes a more liberal view of what might be the space man's intentions.

Helen's suitor Tom Stevens (Hugh Marlowe) shows up to take Helen on a picnic. Klaatu volunteers to look after Bobby while they are gone.

Klaatu and Bobby tour Washington. At Arlington National Cemetery Bobby visits his father's grave and then they go to the Lincoln Memorial where Klaatu says that he would like to talk to a man with the views that are expressed by the Gettysburg Address.

Klaatu takes Bobby to the space ship and explains some of the physics involved in space flight.

Later, Klaatu and Bobby go to Professor Barnhardt's residence and leave him a calling card on his blackboard. Klaatu gives the housekeeper his address and then warns her not to erase the addendum he has placed on the blackboard.

Later a government agent shows up at the rooming house and he and Klaatu leave to go over to Barnhardt's place. Meanwhile, Helen cautions Bobby about becoming too friendly with Klaatu.

There Klaatu tells the professor (Sam Jaffe) that he has to meet with representatives of all the Earth's peoples. Barnhardt suggests that all the scientists might make an appropriate gathering. Klaatu says that he will create a demonstration to show the representatives how crucial it is that they attend.

Back at the rooming house, Stevens tells Helen that he doesn't trust Klaatu. Then they go off to see a movie.

Klaatu asks Bobby for a flashlight because his room lights are out.

Bobby sees that Klaatu's lights are still on and he follows Klaatu to the space ship, where Klaatu signals Gort (Lock Martin) to take out the guards.

Then Klaatu enters the ship and communicates with his home world.

Stevens and Helen return and Bobby tries to tell them about Klaatu and Gort, but they refuse to listen. Stevens goes to Klaatu's room and finds a diamond there. He tells Helen that he thinks Klaatu is up to no good.

The next day Helen is at work, ready for her lunch break when Klaatu appears and tells her that he has to talk to her. They enter an elevator and the power shuts off. Klaatu says that it will be off temporarily and that there is no reason to try to call for assistance.

All across the world the power has been shut down with the exception of aircraft in flight, hospitals and other emergency workers.

Klaatu tells Helen that he has to go to the meeting with the scientists, that the future of the world depends on it.

Meanwhile, Stevens gets an appraisal of the diamond he found in Klaatu's room. It's out of this world he's told.

Helen attempts to get Stevens to forego telling the authorities about Klaatu, but he refuses since he thinks that he will be richly rewarded for exposing Klaatu.

Helen warns Klaatu about Stevens and they take a taxi to go to the meeting. Soldiers have staked out the route they will take.

Klaatu is worried that if he is incapacitated or killed that Gort will be free to destroy Earth. He tells Helen that if he is prevented somehow from the meeting that she must go to Gort and say "Klaatu Birada Nicktoe." She memorizes the phrase as the taxi continues, finally being stopped with Klaatu attempting to escape but he is shot and killed.

Helen goes to Gort. He has been encased in a block of high strength plastic. As soon as she arrives Gort melts the plastic and approaches her. She tries to escape but finally is able to say the magic phrase to Gort. He secretes her in the space ship.

The Army has put Klaatu's body in a secure place, but Gort is able to melt the walls and take Klaatu back to the ship where a machine revives Klaatu.

All the scientists arrive for the meeting and are surprised when the space ship dome opens and Klaatu steps out. He tells them that he's leaving but will keep a careful watch on Earth's activities with atomic weapons. If they find a peaceful means of coexistence then he and their race of robot policemen with unlimited power will not return.

The ship takes off and that ends the film.

William Behr Mueller

Given the extreme tension between the USA and the USSR during the time the picture was made it's not surprising that an external force had to be sought that would tone down the rhetoric of the Cold War. Since the Korean War was going on at the time it only added another aspect of why a peaceful resolution to the world's problems had to be found.

The DVD is worth getting since there are many explanations of how the film was made. Even if you're not a sci-fi buff you'll find this film worth watching.

The Enemy Below

Cinemascope was the perfect technique to show a destroyer escort, USS Haynes, *moving easily through relatively calm water.*

On board sailors groused about the new captain, wondering whether he was up to the job of skipper. Derogatory terms such as "feather merchant" and "doesn't have his sea legs" meant the crew were very unhappy with how the ship was commanded.

One of the officers, Doc (Russell Collins) observes the crew and listens to their disparaging remarks. On the bridge he tells Executive Officer Lt. Ware (Al Hedison) and crew that they should cut the captain some slack since he was still recovering from having a ship he was on torpedoed and sunk.

The radarman finally sees something on his scope. He alerts the bridge, which in turn alerts Captain Murrell (Robert Mitchum).

Murrell makes his way to the bridge amid all of the crew that have assembled to see whether the ship will see some action after all. Murrell questions the radarman as to what the object might be and is told that it might be a submarine. He is told to keep track of the object.

Murrell gets a weather report and heavy weather is moving in.

On the U-boat, Captain Von Stolberg (Curt Jurgens) philosophizes about the war with his second in command Heine Schwaffer (Theodore Bikel). He needs a couple of drinks to be able to sleep. As he finally dozes off, Schwaffer covers him and goes back to the control room.

William Behr Mueller

On the surface Murrell and Doc also philosophize about the ship, the war and the crew. Shortly, the *Haynes* and her crew slog through rain and heavy seas. They still track the U-boat.

On the U-boat Von Stolen is awoken with the information that a ship is within range of their tracking system. They watch the display and Von Stolen has to evaluate the new information. He wants to continue on their present course since it will lead them to a raider that will take the code book they have acquired and thus release them to return to Germany.

When the weather clears the U-boat is spotted and Murrell orders battle stations and flank speed to intercept the U-boat and attempt to sink it.

Von Stolen ups periscope and spots the *Haynes* bearing down on his ship. He orders the submarine to dive and take up a defensive depth.

Murrell makes his attack but is unsuccessful as Von Stolen reverses his course to elude the destroyer escort.

Because Murrell is convinced that the submarine will continue on its course and that he will need more help in trying to destroy the U-boat he sends a message asking for reinforcements.

The additional destroyers will not arrive in time before *Haynes* is brought in range of the raider's guns so Murrell gives his plotter a hypothetical course for the submarine and asks for an intercept point. The plotter gives him the result and Murrell tells his assembled officers and chiefs exactly what he attempts to do: on the hour go in and drop a single pattern of depth charges and continue that pattern to delay the submarine from making good progress toward the raider.

Von Stolen determines that the only way to escape will be to take the submarine to the bottom, which Schwaffer says they cannot do because the hull will implode. Nonetheless, the submarine goes into the red zone on its depth gauge and finally settles to listen to see whether *Haynes* will make any noise, particularly propeller noise that will show that it is leaving.

Murrell tells his ship to wind down the turbines and go silent to deceive the German captain.

Von Stolen listens to the hydrophone to get any hint that *Haynes* is not directly above them waiting for them to surface. After much waiting and listening he finally decides that there is no threat above him.

On board *Haynes* the hydrophone operator hears the propeller noise from the U-boat and informs Murrell who orders sonar to track the submarine.

Von Stolen is at a loss to initiate another plan to escape when he decides that the only solution will be to take advantage of the Hayne's captain making the same mistake of turning to a parallel course after a depth charge run.

Von Stolen has four torpedoes prepared with the hope that one of them will strike *Haynes*.

As Murrell makes his turn, Von Stolen knows that he has predicted the fatal error of the destroyer escort's captain. He fires the torpedoes.

One of the torpedoes hits the *Haynes*.

William Behr Mueller

The rest of the film shows the heroism of both crews and the final humanity of both captains. All the naval procedures give you a feeling that the technical advisor and the US Navy wanted to make sure that all the fictional action was grounded in accurate commands and actions aboard both ships. If this were an Ebert and Siskel review it would get two thumbs up.

The Horse's Mouth

If you're an Alec Guinness fan you won't want to miss this film. He was stationed aboard a ship that had stopped for mechanical problems and he was initially put off by Joyce Cary's writing when the book came out. Years later his wife said that the book might make a good film. The rest is, as they say, history.

A noisy street with a bicyclist riding past London double-decker buses opens the film. The rider is Nosy (Mike Morgan) and he is going to Wormwood Scrubbs penitentiary where Gully Jimson (Alec Guinness) is about to be released.

Jimson comes out and will have nothing to do with Nosy until after scouring a telephone coin return and finding a coin he tells Nosy to get him a packet of fags across the street. While Nosy is engaged Jimson takes Nosy's bicycle and rides off. Nosy and a group of men yell "Stop thief" until a police constable (bobby) joins the run. Nosy has to admit that the bike wasn't stolen and is chastised by the bobby.

Jimson returns to his dilapidated houseboat that some ragamuffins are tearing apart. He tells them not to run off but to stay for lunch.

Inside he lights a match to inspect the painting of Adam and Eve that has a well done foot and calf but when he comes to the serpent's eye he finds that it should have been white instead of red.

Not finding any paint or serviceable brushes he leaves the domicile and goes to another of the red telephone booths and calls his nemesis Hickson (Ernest Thesiger) with a false identity and attempts to get 250 pounds to be able to buy the needed supplies. The butler announces the call and Hickson determines that it's Jimson. He refuses Jimson's attempt at extorting money.

Undaunted Jimson attempts to portray himself as a duchess with a wobbly old woman's voice. Hickson tells the butler to get the police to trace the call. Hickson refuses Jimson again. In his gravel voice Jimson tells Hickson he will cut out his liver and burn his house down.

A bobby shows up at the telephone booth and Jimson is cautioned not to repeat his threat against Hickson's life or property.

Jimson goes to his friend's bar. Dee Coker (Kay Walsh) laments having the face that she's been given while she serves a beer to a sailor (uncredited). A stiff breeze accompanies Jimson's entrance blowing the foam off the sailor's beer.

Jimson and Coker discuss the 4 pounds 13 shillings and 6 pence that he owes Coker. He agrees to go to his ex-wife's place to try to get one of his paintings. Because she might be getting repaid Coker advances Jimson a few shillings to be able to buy supplies. She says that she will be by his houseboat in the morning to pick him up so they can go to the ex-wife's place.

Jimson retouches the Adam and Even painting when Coker arrives. He tells her he's busy but she finally gets him to leave his painting to accompany her to the ex-wife's. He has also received a letter from a patron of the arts asking him to pay a visit for a possible commission.

Coker finds out that Hickson took 19 of Jimson's painting to retire the painter's debt. She tells him that they will go to

Hickson's place to get satisfaction for all the paintings that were gotten for a song.

At Hickson's Jimson attempts to steal a figurine since he tells Coker that the residents never look at it.

Suddenly the noise of a police car is heard and Jimson and Coker flee. They commandeer a cab that is occupied by two proper gentlemen. One (Peter Bull) tells Jimson that if they don't leave the police will be called. Jimson says the police know all about them. Coker cannot take any more of Jimson's escapades and she leaves the cab giving the letter from the patron back to Jimson.

He goes to the building in which the patron lives. A.W. Alabaster (Arthur Macrae) answers the door and Jimson introduces himself.

Inside Jimson sees a wall that he wants. He sees "The Raising of Lazarus" and describes to Alabaster what his vision entails. Alabaster tells Jimson that the 7,000 pound figure he announces might be a bit much for the Beeders. "If they want culture they pay," Jimson responds. They, of course, want a framed painting, but he says he will throw in the wall for nothing.

The Beeders return and have a jolly good time with Jimson who tells them that he will keep the Archbishop of Canterbury waiting while he finishes the painting they desire.

Sir William takes the liberty of telling Jimson that his wife paints. She demurs but he insists that Jimson would want to see her paintings.

Alabaster brings her amateurish paintings for Jimson to view while Sir William gets drinks for all of them. He critiques Sir

William Behr Mueller

William's wife's work while drinking more and more brandy and trying to achieve a sexual conquest of her.

Jimson tells them something "straight from the horse's mouth;" you must know when you've succeeded and when you've failed. He starts to dance and then tells them that he will sleep with Sir William's wife just before he collapses on the floor. So he ultimately inhabits the Beeders bed.

The next morning he finds that they have decamped for a holiday and only the maid is there putting sheets on all the furniture to keep the dust off.

Jimson finds out that the Beeders will be gone for six weeks. He tries to finagle the key from the maid but she reads a note that tells her to give the key to the porter. As the Lieutenant Kije suite fills the soundtrack Jimson goes to the porter to get the key and then with key in hand he takes a clock from the domicile to a pawn shop where he figures the pawn price into the ultimate figure he will receive from the Beeders for the commission.

Nosy shows up at the pawn shop. Jimson gives Nosy some money and tells him to get a tiger.

In the apartment Jimson paints a tiger on the wall and tells Nosy he needs a live tiger. He then discusses what his vision of the painting is with Nosy.

Various models arrive much to the consternation of the porter. They are there to provide feet for Jimson's painting.

Jimson answers the door and Abel (Michael Gough) stands there. Jimson attempts to keep him out but is unsuccessful. Abel tells Jimson that what he sees is almost cause for putting

Jimson away. He looks at the skylight and tells Jimson that he has a commission.

Soon a huge block of stone arrives through the skylight. Jimson tussles with Abel until he tells Abel to "let go." The rigger tells the crane operator to let go and the stone crashes through the floor to the apartment below. Abel finds the milieu of the bottom apartment to be exactly right.

The woman who was Jimson's model is now Abel's nude as he reduces the stone to a shadow of its former shape.

Abel asks for Jimson's opinion. Jimson says it's getting smaller and smaller. Abel climbs the ladder to the upper apartment. "Too many feet," Abel says, "It's a dreadful painting."

Jimson goes into a tirade and then tells himself that Abel was right. "Not the vision that I had." He covers the hole in the floor with a rug and prepares to leave.

Just then the Beeders and Alabaster arrive to see with wide-eyed amazement the wall that Jimson created. As they approach the painting they fall through the hole to the apartment below.

Jimson comes out from behind the door and leaves. He returns to his houseboat. The sailor tells Jimson that it's the monsoon. He tells the sailor to shut up. Seeing smoke from the chimney, Jimson sees that Coker has taken over and cleaned it up. She explains why she has taken over the houseboat. She tells him to take off his clothes and get into bed—without any expectations.

As he lolls in the only bed he tells Coker something of his life. She recounts the good and the bad of her life as Jimson asks her why she prays. In the course of the conversation Jimson finds out that Hickson has died and given his paintings to the national gallery.

Jimson visits the gallery and his ex-wife confronts him. He finds out that she has the picture that he wanted weeks ago. They go to a pub and talk about old times. After a number of refills they go to her place and continue the revelry. Jimson rolls up the painting he's schemed to get but she takes it and puts it into a chest.

Back at the houseboat, Coker and Nosy find out that Jimson has retrieved the painting, but it turns out to be toilet paper rolls. Coker makes good use of the fake painting.

Jimson forces his way into his ex-wife's flat while Nosy attempts to stop the fracas. She falls back and tells him that the painting is hers. Nosy and Jimson escape through a field and wait out the chase in an abandoned niche.

Nosy explores the abandoned building and summons Jimson to look at an even larger wall. It's the inside of a church. "The Last Judgment," Jimson intones.

As the church is scheduled for demolition Jimson hires himself out to give lessons to those who want to paint the wall.

He gives numbered squares to the "students" and has the usual problems with committee work.

The clerk to the surveyor shows up and tells Jimson that the time is short before demolition.

Meanwhile the Beeders and Alabaster have to deal with the publicity of Jimson's painting on their wall. Jimson using his old trick attempts to get Mrs. Beeson to come to the site to the new wall.

At the site, she paints a giraffe to Jimson's praise. Another artist is told that her whale is upside down. He doesn't chastise her as the wrecking crew is ready to go to work.

Everybody watches as the bulldozer cranks up to destroy the wall. It comes down in a flurry of dust. The crowd is saddened and disgusted. Coker recognizes Jimson's cough and he is the one who drove the bulldozer.

Coker bonks the surveyor's clerk and a general melee breaks out.

Jim hurries to his houseboat and tells the sailor to let her go because Jimson is away with the tide. His boat drifts out into the Thames River as Coker and Nosy arrive to the strains of Lt. Kije.

Jimson assesses some of the ships in the river as he passes by.

Nosy provides a fitting tribute to Jimson as his houseboat sails under Tower Bridge.

Happy viewing.

William Behr Mueller

The Sand Pebbles

Jerry Goldsmith (r.i.p.) turned his musical hand at creating "oriental" music as a background for this film. The music leads off in a kind of overture and continues through the opening credits.

As the film opens a graphic identifies the scene as "China 1926" with background material on the situation in that great land mass with multitudes of people. The graphic changes to tell us that we're looking at "Shanghai."

A US Navy jolly boat arrives at the dock and Jake Holman (Steve McQueen) steps off with his sea bag and slings it onto his shoulder. Shirley Eckert (Candice Bergen) looks at Holman as his orders are scrutinized. Holman is told to stay off the streets as there is no liberty. He goes to The Crow's Nest bar. A new owner tells Holman that he can have his share of the gunboats, particularly the *San Pablo* to which Holman has been assigned as engineer. Holman picks up a bar girl.

Meanwhile the *San Pablo* steams into port.

Holman enters the dining room of a ferryboat and is introduced to Eckert and her missionary colleague Mr. Jameson (Larry Gates). The discussion centers around China and the American gunboats.

In the next scene Holman entertains some Chinese children with his butterflies and rabbits. Eckert asks him whether he understood what the men at last night's dinner were talking about. She reveals that she's not a missionary but a teacher. Holman reacts by asking her if she's going to try to teach "the slope heads."

Holman defends being an engineer on a small boat because they leave him alone. Eckert makes small talk by telling Holman that her brother was a lieutenant in the reserve during the war (WWI). He's been in China for 7 years and she says that she's signed up to teach for 7 years. He tells her that as long as she's good at it they "can't bust you down."

When the ferry docks, Jameson explains his view of the China Sailor that Holman represents as Eckert watches Holman hire a rickshaw. Later that evening Holman arrives at the *San Pablo*.

Captain Collins (Richard Crenna) and Frenchy Burgoyne (Richard Attenborough) watch Holman approach the ship. A coolie in a sailor's uniform takes Holman's sea bag. Burgoyne explains that it's the coolie's rice bowl.

Holman goes into the engine compartment and inspects the working parts of the ship's power plant.

Holman sees a Chinese man tending the boiler, but doesn't say anything to him. Instead he goes back to the engine and introduces himself "Hello Engine. I'm Jake Holman."

The next morning, another Chinese blows the wakeup bugle call as Holman is offered coffee by another Chinese man. Holman rolls out of his bunk and the rest of the crew introduce themselves.

Stawski (Simon Oakland) coerces Holman into getting a shave from another Chinese because Holman "doesn't want to break anybody's rice bowl."

The ship's company stands at attention as the flag is raised on the stern to the accompaniment of another bugle call. Captain

William Behr Mueller

Collins dismisses the sailors as a horde of Chinese onlookers enjoy all of the ritual.

The drill for the day is "repel boarders starboard" to which the onlookers clap as it must be one of their favorite activities aboard the ship. Holman mans the steam hose and when all the positions are manned and ready the steam douses the onlookers.

When the drill is complete Holman wants to know how often they do that drill. "Every day but Sunday," Burgoyne says. "What do you do then, turn a machine gun on 'em?" Holman asks.

In the engine compartment, Holman has his first set-to with the "Boss Coolie" when he wants to inspect the bilge plates. He tells the boss that "this ain't the Chinese navy."

The boss blows the glass and inundates Holman with steam. Stawski tells Holman that they couldn't get along without the boss and his coolies. Holman replies that he can get along without them.

Burgoyne explains the coolie situation aboard the *San Pablo*. It is not to Holman's liking.

After a rousing speech by the captain, *San Pablo* gets underway with Holman tending the engine.

Holman notices that one of the engine's bearings is bad and he informs the captain. Maintain speed is his answer. Back in the engine compartment the annunciator asks for full speed. Holman grabs the speaking tube and tells the bridge that the engine won't take any more speed.

Ensign Bordelles (Charles Robinson) comes into the engine room and hears the bad bearing. He orders the ship stopped for repairs.

Holman starts to loosen the nut holding the bearing when the boss coolie pleads that it's his job.

With the engine secured the boss coolie holds the wrench under the crankshaft as two other coolies remove the nut on the other end of the bearing bolt. Unfortunately the jacking mechanism doesn't hold and the boss coolie is severely injured by the rotating crankshaft.

Boss coolie dies and is taken off the ship. Holman is told to clean up as the captain wants to see him.

There is bad blood between Collins and Holman and it will be an ongoing problem for both.

The crew heads for The Crow's Nest as soon as they return to port. Burgoyne asks Holman how he made out with the captain. "We ain't waltzin'," Holman says.

The house madam tells Burgoyne to go upstairs to Maily (Marayat Andriane). He says he will.

Maily comes down the stairs and Stawski takes her over, telling the other sailors to beat it. She tells him in perfect English what her name is. Stawski attempts to take her upstairs but she demurs saying that she is only a hostess.

Burgoyne attempts to free Maily from Stawski but the shore patrol intervenes. Then the madam tells Stawski that if she wants Maily he will have to pay $200. He is floored.

William Behr Mueller

Burgoyne, Holman and Maily take a table after she was rescued by the madam. She finds out that Holman is from Utah and Burgoyne is from Philadelphia. Holman leaves and Burgoyne tells Maily that he will get the $200. and give it to her.

Back at the ship, Holman approaches Po-han (Mako) to be the new boss coolie in the engine room. Po doesn't want to experience the same fate as the previous coolie boss. Holman begins the long process of teaching him the intricacies of the engine room, particularly the difference between live steam and water (dead steam).

Stawski starts to beat Po, but Holman knocks him to the deck.

Lop-eye, the overall coolie boss fires Po-han because of Stawski's perjured testimony. Captain Collins reverses the order and tells Bordelles that it might serve a higher purpose and that will be to make Lop-eye understand his place aboard the ship.

In the crew's quarters Holman wagers that Po can whip Stawski.

Burgoyne meets Maily and tells her what Holman is about. She confesses that she is an orphan and that the man who runs The Crow's Nest paid to have her released and now she has to have enough money to pay him back.

As they talk, Po and Stawski prepare to fight in a makeshift ring. Po is nervous but Stawski is supremely confident, so much so that he drinks beer as he waits to start.

Stawski taunts Po as bets are made. Stawski appears to have the best of Po, making Holman and Burgoyne fear they have started something that will end badly. Stawski looks at Maily and tells her to pack her bags for the trip across the Delaware.

The fight continues with Po getting more banged up, but Stawski appears to be tiring. Finally Po starts to fight and he finishes Stawski just as the whistle recalling the sailors to the ship sounds.

Captain Collins urges the men to get aboard and Holman to get up steam. As they wait the lines are cast off and the ship drifts away from the pier as an angry, torch carrying mob approaches.

Collins explains to Bordelles that there was a battle in which many Chinese were killed when two British gunboats fought with a warlord. The Bolsheviks inflated the number of innocent Chinese killed and thus infuriated the mob that approached the *San Pablo*.

Collins explains the policy that he must operate under and that includes one last trip to the mission at China Light to evacuate the Americans there.

All the personnel except Jameson wait for the ship. Collins sends a jolly boat to fetch Jameson and Eckert.

A contingent of student soldiers meets Bordelles, Holman and Burgoyne at the mission. As Bordelles talks with Jameson, Holman inspects some machinery that is sitting idle. He tells Eckert that their destination and hers are the same. Evidently some opium was found in Jameson's luggage and he was sentenced to death as a result. Now they have to go to the downriver city to appeal the sentence.

Lop-eye sent Po-han ashore and the mob has him. Collins offers ransom but the mob wants to kill Po with the death of a thousand cuts. Po asks to be shot and Holman obliges with a heavy heart. Giving the captain a disdainful look Holman goes to the furnace and starts shoveling coal.

Later, on deck Eckert talks with Holman. She attempts to assuage his grief but he walks away.

Collins berates Holman and forces him to request a transfer. Meanwhile he will continue to run the ship's engine.

Holman steps onto the deck as the ship sails on.

An intermission starts at this point (about half way through the film).

San Pablo arrives at its destination only to face numerous sampans with signs that read "Go Home."

Collins replies to the demands that they can "go to hell." He orders the hose to disperse the boats.

The missionaries go ashore accompanied by an armed escort from the ship. At the mission, Bordelles confronts Major Chin (Richard Loo) who has taken over part of the mission for his headquarters. Chin forces the Navy to retreat under the escort of his men. The crowd jeers the men and throw old vegetables and other detritus on them.

The sailors clean up and then go back to The Crow's Nest. Burgoyne gives Holman the money to buy Maily's freedom. The civilians don't want to see Maily freed and they bid up the price. And then they propose an auction for Maily.

The bidding rises and then Holman can't take stripping Maily. He wades into the civilians and a general melee starts. The lights go out and Burgoyne, Holman and Maily escape.

Burgoyne talks with Maily in a secluded room, convincing her not to return to The Crow's Nest. She, in turn, convinces Burgoyne to stay.

On the way back to the ship Burgoyne tells Holman that he wants to marry Maily. Holman reminds him that it's impossible.

Holman buys a caged bird for Eckert and she releases it. At an elephant statue Holman tosses a coin and it sticks and he gives his wish to Eckert. She says that she wished he would tell her more about himself.

Sitting in a rowboat Holman tells her a lot about himself and how he joined the Navy.

Burgoyne marries Maily with Holman and Eckert as witnesses. It is not the usual ceremony. Eckert goes to Holman and he kisses her. She tries to talk Holman into returning with her to China Light. He reminds her that he told her not to talk to sailors.

At the elephant Holman hears the alarm horn from the ship. As the sailors return they see all the coolies jumping ship.

The San Pablo is under siege and will remain so all winter. There will be no liberty except for a once a week mail run.

A Junk sails by with the missionaries aboard. Holman goes to the bow of the ship to watch the Junk sail away.

The seasons pass and Burgoyne decides to jump ship. He becomes very ill with Maily at his side. She reveals that she's pregnant.

Holman leaves the ship with a packet for the consul in Changsha. He wears a pistol. He goes to see Burgoyne and finds him dead. Holman fights with some Chinese thugs who take Maily and Burgoyne's body.

Sampans approach the ship demanding Holman who they say is a murderer. Maily is the victim. Holman tells Collins that he didn't think they would do that.

Collins prepares to take the ship away from Changsha. The crew confront Holman and demand that he gives himself up to Chinese justice. Stawski is particularly nasty.

Chinese nationalist soldiers demand that Holman be surrendered. Members of the crew start a chant to make Holman come down to be surrendered to the soldiers.

Collins fires a burst in front of the soldiers and that quells the nascent mutiny. Collins goes to his cabin and contemplates suicide.

Bordelles reads a message that Nationalist forces have taken Shanghai and that American lives are in danger. Collins tells them that the radio is out of order and therefore they are on their own. He plans to go to China Light and rescue the missionaries.

The ship moves through the water advancing toward a boom guarded by soldiers. It is the captain's decision to break the boom and rescue the people at China Light.

The battle begins with all stations manned and ready. The ship steers for the center junk.

Boarding parties fight and kill many of the boom guard force. Holman grabs an axe and chops the boom. He has to use his axe to defend himself and it is traumatic to see the man who was attacking him die with an axe wound.

The ship moves forward with the men tending to their wounds.

That night the captain and an armed escort go to China Light. He finds out that Jameson and Eckert have declared themselves "stateless persons." Collins and Jameson argue the merits of Chinese justice.

Holman tells the Captain to leave. He says that it's desertion in the face of the enemy.

Soldiers appear. Jameson attempts to tell them that he's stateless, they kill him. The battle for survival is on.

Collins attempts to make a last stand, but he is killed. Holman goes back to aid Collins.

Eckert and two other sailors leave Holman to fight alone. He is shot right next to the machinery that he was going to install for Eckert. Holman dies alone.

The others make it back to the ship.

As the San Pablo steams off under the command of Bordelles, the film ends.

Not a happy ending, but considering how many died in the Chinese civil war it was amazing that the US was not dragged into it directly. This film will give you a wave's eye view of the civil war, the way of the Chinese and how difficult it was for men in the US Navy to live and work among the disparate points of view held by almost everybody in the country.

The Third Man

Haven't heard a zither before? You're in for a real treat. Anton Karas plays the main theme as the credits run. You'll also hear "The Café Mozart Waltz" later in the film.

As the film opens a graphic identifies the scene as "Vienna" and a voice over says that he's never seen the old Vienna, the Vienna that was there before the war (World War II).

Describing the black market and the division of the city into four zones: American, British, French and Russian with the usual language barriers the narrator continues by saying that he was going to tell us the story of Holly Martins, a friend of Harry Lime. Martins was broke and Lime had offered him a job. The voiceover ends with a train pulling into the station in the western zone.

Martins (Joseph Cotten) gets off the train and is asked by an occupation soldier what the purpose of his visit is. Martins answers that a friend Harry Lime (Orson Welles) offered him a job and he will be staying with Lime.

Martins goes to Lime's address and a porter speaking German tells him that he's ten minutes too late.

In broken English Karl the porter (Paul Horbiger) tells Martins that Lime's friends and the coffin have already left. Martins wonders about the coffin. Karl continues with the explanation that Lime was hit by a car and is already in Hell (pointing upward) or in Heaven (downward).

Martins goes to the graveyard and inquires of a bystander, Major Calloway (Trevor Howard) who is being buried. It's Lime.

Some of the attendees pay particular attention to Martins as he looks at Anna Schmidt (Valli).

After tossing some earth onto the grave all the attendees leave. Calloway offers Martins a ride back to town. The car passes by Schmidt as Calloway turns to look at her.

Arriving at a bar, Calloway finds out that Martins knew Lime for some time and then when Martins tells Calloway that Lime was the best friend he ever had, Calloway says that sounds like a cheap novelette. Martins tells Calloway that he writes cheap novelettes such as *The Lone Rider of Santa Fe* or *Death at Double X Ranch*. Calloway says he hasn't read either.

When Martins laments Lime's death, Calloway tells him that Lime was a dirty racketeer. Martins tells Calloway that he should be catching murderers not petty racketeers. Martins attempts to land a punch on Calloway, but Sgt. Paine (Bernard Lee) grabs Martins and moves him out of the way. When Paine hears Martins name he asks whether he's the Martins who wrote *Death at Double X Ranch?*

Calloway gives Martins some money and says they will keep a seat for him on the morning's plane. Martins attempts another shot at Calloway and Paine decks Martins telling him to be careful.

Paine takes Martins to the military hotel telling him that he likes westerns because he can pick them up and put them down any time.

As Martins is registering Paine goes over to Crabbin (Wilfred Hyde-White) and tells him that he's a good author even though Crabbin has never heard of him.

William Behr Mueller

Crabbin makes Martins a deal he can't refuse and provides Martins with the ability to stay in Vienna to sort out Lime's death.

Martins gets a phone call from Baron Kurtz (Ernst Deutsch). He was a friend of Lime's. They agree to meet at the Mozart Café just around the corner from the hotel. Kurtz will carry a copy of one of Martins books (Oklahoma Kid), given to him by Lime.

Kurtz makes light of Lime's involvement in the black market with the oft stated phrase that "everybody does it." Martins asks Kurtz to help him clear up Lime's death, but Kurtz demurs saying that he's an Austrian and has to be careful with the police.

After the meeting, Kurtz takes Martins back to where Lime was killed and explains how it happened. Karl the porter listens to Kurtz as Karl's wife cleans a window.

Kurtz tells Martins that only he and a Romanian Mr. Popescu (Siegfried Breuer) were at Lime's side when he died. Martin says that Karl said he died instantly. Kurtz hedges by saying that he died before the ambulance could arrive.

Martins goes over to Karl as Kurtz translates. Kurtz says that Karl didn't know everybody who visited Lime. Then Karl's wife insists that he go back inside for "the telephone." Kurtz mentions Dr. Winkel as Martins asks about the attendees at the funeral. Kurtz says that Lime was a playboy and that accounted for Schmidt being at the funeral. She works at the Josefstadt theater.

Martins goes to the theater and talks with Schmidt. She tells him that Lime's doctor and his driver both were at the scene. Martins finds the coincidence hard to swallow.

They go to Lime's flat and talk to Karl about Lime. He tells them that he heard but didn't see the accident. Karl says that there was a third man who didn't give evidence at the inquest. Karl says the man might have been "anybody."

Schmidt answers the phone but no one answers.

Martins attempts to get Karl to go to the police, but Karl says it was an accident and that Martins is up to no good according to Karl's wife. As they argue, a ball bounces into the room followed by a boy. Karl tells them to leave.

At Schmidt's domicile, her landlady (Hedwig Bleibtreu) tells Schmidt that the police are there asking about her. Calloway asks to see Schmidt's papers. Paine also examines the pass and determines that it's a forgery. Paine also takes letters to Schmidt from Lime.

Calloway leaves with Schmidt in tow.

At headquarters, a Russian officer examines Schmidt's papers.

Martins goes to Dr. Winkel's residence. Winkel (Eric Ponto) is having a dinner party. The result of the visit is that Winkel cannot render an opinion since he didn't see the accident.

Back at headquarters a Russian officer says he will make inquires about Schmidt. Calloway asks Schmidt whether she knows Joseph Harbin, a worker in a military hospital. She says she doesn't know him. Calloway tells her that Harbin disappeared the day she phoned him. Calloway needs to find Harbin.

At the Casanova club Crabbin tells Martins that he's arranged for him to speak on the modern novel at the Wednesday meeting. Martins doesn't have the foggiest idea of what Crabbin is talking about, but agrees to be there for the meeting.

Martins meets Schmidt as Kurtz serenades one of the patrons. Kurtz tells Martins that Popescu is back in Vienna.

Popescu gives his version of Lime's death, but Martins doesn't buy it. Martins asks whether Popescu knows Joseph Harbin. He gets a negative answer.

Kurtz, Winkel and Popescu meet someone at a bridge.

Meanwhile Martins goes back to the street where Lime was killed. He talks with Karl and says he will return that evening. Karl turns from the window and is frightened by what he sees.

Schmidt sits alone in her flat. Martins arrives and tries to help her with a part she has to learn. It's a washout since he cannot pronounce the German words. Schmidt is depressed and asks Martins to talk about Lime.

They leave her flat and go back to see Karl. There is a crowd around the building. Martins finds out that Karl has been killed. The same boy who was in an earlier scene chases after Martins and Schmidt as the crowd gives chase convinced that Martins is the killer.

Martins and Schmidt find refuge in a theater. Schmidt leaves to return to her place. Martins walks out and gets a taxi driven by a disreputable looking driver.

The cab careens around the streets finally arriving at the Wednesday meeting with Crabbin.

As Martins struggles with the questions from the audience, Popescu sets up a meeting that may have dire consequences for Martins.

Popescu questions Martins about whether he's working on a new book. Martins replies that he is and it's a murder mystery based on fact. Then, Popescu meets two thugs and the chase is on. Martins runs up the stairs and finally escapes through a window after being bitten by a parrot.

Running through the ruins Martins finally finds an abandoned car to hide in.

He goes back to Calloway who tells Paine to get the Lime file. With magic lantern pictures (slides) Martins sees the rack and ruin that Lime created with his black market activity in diluted penicillin.

Martins leaves convinced that Lime is guilty. The Russian officer asks Calloway for Schmidt's passport.

At a bar, Martins drinks and then buys a bouquet. He goes to Schmidt's place. Trying to get a cat to play Martins finds out that the cat only liked Lime. Schmidt knows about Lime's nefarious activities, too.

A shadowy figure appears in the street below Schmidt's flat. He ducks into a doorway. The cat finds the man and nestles against his shoes.

Schmidt and Martins trade barbs about their lives and how they entwine with Lime's.

Martins leaves and confronts the man in the shadows. A light comes on illuminating the man's face. It's Harry Lime. Martins attempts to talk to Lime who runs off, disappearing in the middle of a street.

Martins leads Calloway and Paine to where he lost Lime. They determine that Lime escaped through the sewer entrance in the middle of the street.

They go into the Viennese sewer system.

Then they return to Lime's grave and find Joseph Harbin in the coffin.

As Calloway and Martins leave the graveyard, members of the International Police go to Schmidt's place and take her into custody.

At police headquarters, Calloway interviews Schmidt and tells her that Harbin's body was in Lime's coffin. She is happy that Lime is alive but has no idea where he is.

Martins tells Kurtz that he will wait at the big Ferris Wheel to talk to Harry. Harry shows up and talks to Martins on board the wheel. Martins digs into Lime with news of Schmidt. Lime says he can do nothing. Lime opens the door to the car and asks Martins whether he would feel any pity if "one of those dots down there stopped moving?" Lime proposes an alliance with Martins, but to no avail. Lime philosophizes about the Borgias and the wars with the Renaissance while the peaceful Swiss produced the cuckoo clock.

Back at police headquarters Calloway attempts to get Martins to rat Lime out. Martins only finally agrees if Schmidt can be relieved of her immigration problem.

Schmidt is ready to take a train out of Vienna when she discovers that Martins has sold Lime for her ability to leave. She dismisses the chance to leave and Martins is crushed that he has betrayed Lime for nothing.

Calloway takes Martins to see Lime's victims and it is horrifying to Martins who agrees to help Calloway track Lime down.

Martins is going to meet Lime in a Café. As they wait a balloon vendor interrupts the stake-out.

Schmidt enters the café, confronts Martins and tells him that Kurtz and the others have been arrested. As Lime approaches, Schmidt warns Lime that it is a trap. Lime runs away. The police pursue Lime in the Viennese sewers.

More police arrive to aid the chase. Lime runs from one tunnel to another trying to find a way out, but the grates that usually lead to the street have been shuttered. He cannot escape. He shoots Paine.

Martins finally finds Lime in his last effort trying to lift a grate. Martins shoots his friend with Paine's pistol, administering the coup de grace and finally ending Harry Lime's life.

At the graveyard Lime is laid to rest. Calloway agrees to help Schmidt if she will let him.

Martins gets out of the Jeep and waits for Schmidt who walks past him without an acknowledgement.

This film has a little bit of everything for everybody: mystery for the aficionados, love for the Eros stricken, police work for the procedural minded and justice for those who yearn for it. If that weren't enough it's hugely entertaining as well.

The Usual Suspects

Who is Kiser Sose? That becomes the central question in this unusual of usual suspect mysteries. Be prepared for heavy duty street language and a surprise ending that will be water cooler material for days and perhaps weeks. John Ottman's strange sounds play behind the front credits (he also edited the film).

A graphic indicates that we're looking at San Pedro, California— last night.

Dean Keaton (Gabriel Byrne) strikes a matchbook as he sits against some boxes aboard a ship. He lights a cigarette and then drops the matches onto a stream of flammable fluid that ignites and races past a body as the camera pans up to a figure pissing on the flames.

The shrouded figure walks down stairs, stands in front of Keaton and lights a cigarette with a lighter. Keaton stares up at him but says nothing. The figure asks how he's doing. He says he can't feel his legs and then calls the figure "Kiser." He finds the time to be 12:30 and then the figure shoots Keaton twice.

Various shots show the ship and its name "Tanager." The figure drops his cigarette into the liquid that ignites again. We also see something behind a stack of cordage but it's hidden.

As the ship explodes we dissolve to an interrogation of Roger "Verbal" Kint (Kevin Spacey). He says it all started six weeks ago when a truck was hijacked.

A graphic tells us that we are looking at New York City—six weeks ago.

The police awake Michael McManus (Stephen Baldwin) and arrest him.

We see a paint shaker in action as lawmen enter the building and ask Todd Hockney (Kevin Pollack) if that's his name. He wipes his brow and asks if they've brought enough guys.

Fred Fenster (Benicio Del Toro) evades police on a street, but they nab him.

Keaton is sitting in an upscale restaurant making a pitch to potential investors about his idea for a restaurant that changes with the taste of the times. Dave Kujan, US Customs (Chazz Palminteri) approaches Keaton. They want to talk to Keaton about a small matter of a truck loaded with guns. He leaves his guests with Edie Finneran (Suzy Amis) and accompanies Kujan and the New York policemen.

Kint continues his tale saying that it didn't make sense that he was in jail with hard core hijackers, but there he was. They all appear in a lineup and are told to repeat the phrase they've been given. The phrase doesn't come out the way the police intended.

Individual interrogations follow regarding the hijacked truck. Kint's voice over elaborates on each character as the interrogations continue.

All the men are placed in a group holding cell. They argue and try to determine that there is no probable cause to hold them. Keaton says they're making him tired.

They discuss why they're in the cell and Keaton tells them that it's a setup. The focus turns on Kint who says he got his nickname because he talks too much. Keaton defends him.

McManus wants to save a little dignity and he tells that that he and Fenster heard about a little job. Keaton doesn't want to hear it. In fact he wants nothing to do with any of them. Kint continues his narration about what he found out: these men would never break.

Another graphic tells us that we're back in San Pedro—present day.

Body bags line the deck of the ship we saw at the beginning. Jack Baer, FBI (Giancarlo Esposito) asks how many dead—15 so far the cop replies. One survivor is in county hospital. The other is a crippled guy being interviewed by the D.A. Baer tosses his cigar as the camera pans up to show the ship burning.

A jet readies for landing as Kujan tells someone on the other end of his phone connection that he'll be in LA for a few days.

At police headquarters, Kujan wants to see Kint, but Sgt. Jeff Rabin (Dan Hedaya) puts him off because of internal politics. Rabin says Kint must be protected by the Prince of Darkness. Kujan finds out that Kint will post bail in two hours. Kujan argues with Rabin to at least talk to Kint.

At the hospital Baer wants to talk to the other survivor. In a room the survivor mumbles in Hungarian as Baer tries to get someone to interpret. The name the man repeats is "Kiser Sose."

Back in Rabin's office Kint examines the posters on the wall as he waits for Kujan who is checking his wire to be able to record the interview with Kint.

Kujan takes Kint back to the lineup in New York. Kint provides graphic details of why he needs a cup of coffee. As Rabin leaves for coffee, Kint relates how he was in a barbershop quartet in Skokie, Illinois. Kujan tells Kint that they're trying to help him. He appreciates the effort. Kint relates how Keaton was a cop, but Kujan doesn't buy it. Kint tries to light a cigarette but fumbles the lighter as Kujan tries to get him to reveal something about what if anything he has to do with the massacre aboard the ship. Kujan blackmails Kint with the possibility of telling someone inside the jail that Kint will enter for a weapons charge that he revealed a name to the D.A.

Kujan tells Kint that he's smarter than Kint. Kint replies that he's not a rat. Rabin enters with coffee. Kint relates a story about picking beans in Guatemala. Kujan asks what happened after the lineup.

The scene shifts to New York and the aftermath of the lineup. Keaton talks to Edie about the restaurant deal. Keaton is ready to give up as Kint walks by. As Edie pleads her love, Keaton looks at the other guys across the street from the police station.

Kint describes the job that McManus talked about earlier. To do it right will take five men.

Keaton puts Kint up against a wall in Edie's apartment and Kint tells him that he has to come because without him Kint will not be allowed to go along for the special job. Kint says he has a way to do the job without killing anyone. Keaton is torn between knowing that the cops will never give up even if he does and wanting to score a big one.

Another jet prepares to land. A smuggler (Paul Bartel) leaves the terminal and gets into the NYPD police car. Kint relates the corruption that allowed smugglers to pay the cops as a taxi service.

William Behr Mueller

The heist is on as the police car is boxed it and the men go to work on getting the loot from the smuggler as well as implicating the cops so they will be arrested by internal affairs. The leave as the police car erupts in a ball of fire.

Kint continues his narrative about how the NYPD had the corruption exposed from the chief on down.

The thieves talk about the fence and McManus says that he always has to go to him. The agreement is that they all go to California to see the fence.

First, Keaton has to see Edie before they leave. She is conferring with a client as Keaton looks on.

Back in Rabin's office he makes a sarcastic remark to Kint's tale. Kujan asks him to wait outside. Kujan proceeds to describe Keaton's transgressions while he was on the force before he was remanded to Sing Sing prison for five years.

Agent Baer convinces the hospital staff to allow him and the translator to talk to the survivor. The man demands guarantees because he saw the Devil and looked him in the eye. He then tells a police artist what Kiser Sose looked like.

Kujan tells Kint how he found the supposedly dead Keaton. Then Kujan erupts in a fury and berates Kint with all the negative possibilities that could occur if he doesn't tell Kujan what he wants to know. Kint mentions the lawyer Kobayashi (Pete Postlethwaite).

The scene shifts to California and the meeting with the fence, Redfoot. He tells the guys that he needs men to make a hit. He will keep the merchandise and they get the green. It doesn't go well because Keaton killed a friend of Redfoot.

After a day of McManus nagging Keaton they were back to criminal work.

In a garage they face some men who have a case with the merchandize and cash. The men don't give up easily and McManus has to kill two of them. As Keaton tries to get the case Kint shoots the man with it. The case is filled with dope.

They go back to the rendezvous and wait for Redfoot and his minions. The upshot of the meeting is that the Limey who set up the hit wants to meet Keaton and company.

Back at police headquarters Kujan meets Baer. Baer tells him that there was no dope in the ship and that the man he interviewed mentioned Kiser Sose.

Kujan confronts Kint and asks him who Kiser Sose is.

The scene shifts to a hotel with all the men arguing about Redfoot. Kobayashi enters the room and says that his employer has sent a proposal to the men. Keaton learns that the lawyer works for Kiser Sose. Kobayashi proceeds to list the infractions that the men committed that impacted Kiser Sose. Since the men didn't know they were stealing from Sose they were not killed, but now they have a way to repay the debit they owe Sose.

Sose wants the men to stop the 91 million dollar narcotics deal, which will alleviate his competition. Keaton threatens Kobayashi who leaves a case on the pool table as a gift from Sose. The case contains blueprints for the ship and envelopes with each of their names. The envelopes contain complete histories of the men. Kint asks who is Kiser Sose.

William Behr Mueller

Continuing his narrative to Kujan, Kint explains who Kiser Sose is. Kint explains that the greatest trick the Devil ever pulled was convincing the world he didn't exist. Kint elaborates on Sose and how he defeated a gang of Turks by shooting his own wife to show that there was nothing he wouldn't do to avenge his honor. Not only his wife but his kids, too. Letting the last Hungarian go he waits until the family is in the ground and then goes after the Hungarians, man, woman and child. After the reign of terror, Sose disappears to become a myth, a spook story.

Kujan asks Kint whether he believes in Sose. Kint counters by saying that Keaton always said he didn't believe in God but he was afraid of him. Kint says he believes in God and the only thing that scares him is Kiser Sose.

Baer tells Rabin that he can get him a file on Sose from another agent who's been working on him for a couple of years.

Kint tells Kujan that he's been upfront about what happened. Kujan attempts to get Kint to turn state's evidence. Kint counters that Kujan can't protect him and that once Sose takes care of Kint he won't be heard from again.

At the hospital the police artist continues the sketch of Sose based on what the survivor says.

Kint tells of Fenster's leaving with some of the money they'd stolen. Kujan asks what happened then. Kobayashi told the men where they could find Fenster. He's dead in a cave. McManus tells them that they have to bury Fenster. Keaton starts to dig the grave.

Kujan asks why they didn't run. Kint says they planned to take out Kobayashi.

The men wait for Kobayashi to take the elevator up to the floor where he will meet Edie. McManus is on top of the elevator and assassinates Kobayashi's two bodyguards. The elevator goes to the 20th floor.

Keaton tells Kobayashi that now he knows they can get to him. Kobayashi brings up the business he has with Miss Finneran. That tidbit stops McManus from shooting him.

At his office Kobayashi makes the men aware that a gruesome fate awaits their relatives and Edie if they don't carry out the raid on the ship.

At the harbor the men evaluate the ship and the potential raid. They wait until dark.

Men speaking a foreign language exit a building next to the ship while on its roof McManus sets up a sniper position with a rifle equipped with a telescopic sight.

Hockney watches a van drive up and a number of men go to the back of the van.

Keaton tells Kint to stay where they are. If they don't get out of the raid alive he wants Kint to take the money and go. He tells Kint to tell Edie that he tried.

Keaton walks onto the dock and up to the men guarding the ship. Hockney tosses a bomb. Shortly the bomb explodes, McManus and Keaton kill the men on the dock and the fight is on.

William Behr Mueller

Hockney shoots many of the men aboard the ship while McManus hand over hands on a rope to the ship. Keaton shoots a threat to Hockney and then climbs aboard the ship.

Hockney opens the van and spies the money and then he's shot as McManus and Keaton eliminate the rest of the crew.

Kujan asks Kint why he didn't run. Froze up is Kint's reply. Kujan tells him that there was no dope on that boat.

A man in a stateroom tells a member of the crew that he knows Kiser Sose is there. The crew member tells him to stay put.

Keaton and McManus meet in the engine room. Keaton says there's no coke.

The man in the stateroom sees someone and tells the person that he told them nothing. It does him no good as he is shot.

Keaton signals Kint as McManus comes on deck, collapses with a knife in his back.

Kint goes to the van, sees Hockney's body and tries to find the keys to the van. Keaton is shot by the shadowy figure we saw at the beginning of the film.

Kujan tells Kint that's what he said in his statement. Kujan becomes abusive to Kint as he tries to get the truth about Keaton. Kint admits that he didn't help Keaton because he was afraid.

At the pier Kint hides behind the stack of cordage that we saw earlier in the film. He watches the scene between the shadowy figure and Keaton.

Kujan tells Kint that the man in the stateroom had seen and could positively identify Kiser Sose. Kujan continues with the story of a hit, a suicide mission to wipe out the one guy who could identify Kiser Sose. Kujan believes that Keaton is Kiser Sose. He was the one man who could kill Edie Finneran, found yesterday in a hotel in Pennsylvania shot twice in the head.

Kint breaks down and admits that everything was Keaton's doing. Kujan tells Kint that he posted bail twenty minutes ago. Kint leaves the office.

The surprise ending comes in three parts: the sketch from the hospital, Kujan's discovery about Kint's stories and what happens outside police headquarters.

For a low budget movie this one has everything that a viewer could want: a plot that keeps you on the edge, characters that are also edgy and interesting, and a story that has as many twists and turns as a bucketful of eels. Watch it and experience real movie going pleasure.

About the Author

I live and write in Sacramento. My wife, Jerrilee, reads exams from prospective elementary teachers.

As a freelancer I've written over a hundred articles and stories in national magazines. I've worked at various companies writing user manuals, operator guides and reports.

Being a one-man publishing business requires more work than the initial writing. Having had experience with other publishers where structure didn't come out exactly as written, the ins and outs of independent publishing are much less onerous and they avoid the irritating and time-consuming faux pas at the other end of the line.

As you can see my fiction is wide ranging, another benefit of indie publishing. A traditional publisher would want a pigeonhole and production, neither of which is appealing.

If you read any of my books, either feel free to drop me a line or write a review on Amazon. And if you want to find out what's coming next visit my website:

http://www.williambehrmueller.com.

www.ingramcontent.com/pod-product-compliance
Lightning Source LLC
Chambersburg PA
CBHW070909290526
45795CB00001B/260